FAHRENHEIT 451

Student Workbook
& Study Guide

Study Questions
Vocabulary Worksheets
Elements Of Fiction
Writing Assignments

Get the most out of what you read with this comprehensive resource for studying literature.
Improve your reading, writing, vocabulary, and other essential skills.

COPYRIGHT INFORMATION

This is copyrighted material.

The purchaser may copy the student materials
for his or her classroom use only.
It may not be copied or distributed for any other purpose
without written permission from the publisher.

No portion may be posted on the Internet
without written permission from the publisher.

Copyright violations are prosecuted to the fullest extent of the law
and are subject to a minimum of a $500.00 fine,
imposed by the publisher
in addition to any other legal judgments obtained.

ISBN 978-1-60249-712-2
Copyright 2014
All Rights Reserved

TABLE OF CONTENTS
STUDENT WORKBOOK
Fahrenheit 451

5	**How To Use This Workbook**
7	**Reading Assignment 1**
9	Character Notes Reading Assignment 1
10	Events and Points of Interest Reading Assignment 1
11	Vocabulary Reading Assignment 1
15	Study Questions Reading Assignment 1
18	Passages for Discussion Reading Assignment 1
19	Comic Strip Characters
20	Clarisse's Poem
21	Back In The Day
23	What's In Your Window?
24	Reader Response Reading Assignment 1
27	**Reading Assignment 2**
29	Character Notes Reading Assignment 2
30	Events and Points of Interest Reading Assignment 2
31	Vocabulary Reading Assignment 2
35	Study Questions Reading Assignment 2
38	Passages for Discussion Reading Assignment 2
39	Play The Man, Master Ridley
40	Books, Books, Books
41	KWL Reading Assignment 2
42	Reader Response Reading Assignment 2
43	**Reading Assignment 3**
45	Character Notes Reading Assignment 3
46	Events and Points of Interest Reading Assignment 3
47	Vocabulary Reading Assignment 3
51	Study Questions Reading Assignment 3
55	Passages for Discussion Reading Assignment 3
57	Dover Beach
58	TV Favorites
59	Judging A Candidate
60	KWL Reading Assignment 3
61	Reader Response Reading Assignment 3
63	**Reading Assignment 4**
65	Character Notes Reading Assignment 4
66	Events and Points of Interest Reading Assignment 4
67	Vocabulary Reading Assignment 4
71	Study Questions Reading Assignment 4
73	Passages for Discussion Reading Assignment 4
75	Ecclesiastes
76	KWL Reading Assignment 4
77	Reader Response Reading Assignment 4

TABLE OF CONTENTS (continued)
STUDENT WORKBOOK
Fahrenheit 451

79	**Writing Assignments**
87	**Whole Book Study**
89	Historical Context
91	Point of View
92	Story Map
93	Plot Diagram
94	Setting & Conflict
95	Character Development
104	Character Comparison
106	Character Traits
109	Symbolism & Imagery
114	Article Evaluation
123	Themes
130	Exploration of Additional Themes
132	Use of Language
138	Figurative Language
140	Unit Crossword
142	Vocabulary Crossword

HOW TO USE THIS STUDENT WORKBOOK
Fahrenheit 451

This workbook contains assignments, graphic organizers, study questions, vocabulary work, writing assignments, and more to help you get the most out of reading *Fahrenheit 451* by Ray Bradbury.

Before you begin a reading assignment:
- **Read through the materials in this workbook for that section of the novel.**
- **Complete the Vocabulary Work for that section of the novel.**

This will give you a "heads up" about what will be important in the reading assignment and alert your brain ahead of time to look for certain information and will help prepare you to understand what you are reading.

As you read:
- **Make notes on the AS YOU READ Character and Events and Points of Interest pages in your workbook.**

This will help you remember what you have read and give you notes to refer to and study. You might be able to do this as you read through the first time, but the best way to do this is to read through the assignment first, and then go back and make notes on the workbook pages. **You will be surprised how much more you will discover and remember if you take the time to read each assignment a second time.**

After you read the assignment:
- **Prepare answers for the STUDY & DISCUSSION QUESTIONS.**

These workbook pages point out important ideas presented in the text. Your teacher may have more specific directions about how and when these pages are to be completed.

Throughout this book study, you will have a variety of additional assignments. Your teacher will tell you which of the additional assignments in this workbook you will be responsible to complete and by when they must be completed.

A Final Note:
As with most things in life, you will get out of this unit what you put into it. If you do the assignments in a timely manner with care and your best efforts, you will be rewarded with knowledge and skills that will help you in life.

Relevance:
Most people who have heard anything about *Fahrenheit 451* think of it as "about book burning and censorship." But a careful reading of this novel reveals so much more. It is a book about what causes a society to degenerate and collapse. It is a warning to all generations about the dangers of giving up responsibility and active participation in life. It is a herald of the consequences of seeking happiness in the wrong places. And, like Clarisse subtly challenges Montag in the novel, this book challenges us to evaluate our own lives and our own society.

NOTES
Fahrenheit 451

READING ASSIGNMENT 1
Fahrenheit 451

THIS ASSIGNMENT COVERS APPROXIMATELY
THE FIRST HALF OF CHAPTER ONE:
"THE HEARTH AND THE SALAMANDER"

START:
Beginning of chapter one

END:
Read through the end of the paragraph beginning
"And, then, Clarisse was gone."

NOTES
Fahrenheit 451

CHARACTER NOTES
Reading Assignment 1 Fahrenheit 451

As you read Assignment 1 use this graphic organizer to jot down information about characters.

MONTAG

CLARISSE

MILDRED

BEATTY

EVENTS & POINTS OF INTEREST
Reading Assignment 1 Fahrenheit 451

As you read Assignment 1 make notes of the series of main events that take place. Put them in the order that they are given in the text.

_____

_____

_____

_____

_____

_____

_____

OTHER POINTS OF INTEREST TO IDENTIFY OR KNOW THE SIGNIFICANCE OF:

Seashells

The sleeping pills

The parlor walls

The Hound

VOCABULARY WORK FOR ASSIGNMENT 1
Fahrenheit 451

PART I: Using Prior Knowledge And Contextual Clues

Use any clues you can find in the sentences from the text combined with your prior knowledge and write what you think the bold word means.

1. With his symbolic helmet number 451 on his **stolid** head...he flicked the igniter and the house jumped up in a gorging fire.

   _____

2. Impossible: for how many people did you know that **refracted** your own light to you.

   _____

3. And if the muscles of his jaws stretched **imperceptibly**, she would yawn long before he would.

   _____

4. He felt that the stars had been **pulverized** by the sound of the black jets and that in the morning the earth would be covered with their dust like a strange snow.

   _____

5. And the men with the cigarettes in their straight-lined mouths, the men with the eyes of puff adders, took up their load of machine and tube, their case of liquid **melancholy** and the slow dark sludge of nameless stuff, and strolled out the door.

   _____

6. Light flickered on bits of ruby glass and on sensitive **capillary** hairs in the nylon-brushed nostrils of the creature...

   _____

7. Below, the Hound had sunk back down upon its eight incredible insect legs and was humming to itself again, its **multifaceted** eyes at peace.

   _____

8. It's like a lesson in **ballistics**. It has a trajectory we decide on for it.

   _____

Vocabulary Work For Fahrenheit 451 Assignment 1, Page 2

PART II: Matching
Considering the usage in Part I, match the vocabulary words to their definitions.

_____ 1. stolid   A. Sadness; gloominess

_____ 2. refracted   B. The study of the dynamics of projectiles

_____ 3. imperceptibly   C. Having or revealing little emotion

_____ 4. pulverized   D. Having many faces, sides, or dimensions

_____ 5. melancholy   E. Deflected from a straight path

_____ 6. capillary   F. Without being detected by ordinary senses

_____ 7. multifaceted   G. Fine; small in diameter

_____ 8. ballistics   H. Reduced to powder

Part III: Cloze Passage
Fill in the blanks with the appropriate vocabulary words from the list above.

The _____ colonel got ready for the testing of the latest army weapon. The missile with its _____ capabilities could not be _____ from a target no matter how an enemy might try to deflect it. The _____ behind the new invention were impressive, with the triggering mechanism being _____ in size. When fired, the missile would race _____ towards its target, which soon would be _____ upon impact. Though a complete success in design and function, a certain _____ fell over the observers as they thought how deadly such a weapon would be and how unsuspecting would be its victims.

Vocabulary Work For Fahrenheit 451 Assignment 1, Page 3

PART IV: Words In Practice
Answer the questions and be able to give short explanations to justify your answers.

1. If someone has a stolid reaction to what has happened, is that person excited about the results or unaffected by them?

    _____

2. If an object thrown at you is refracted, are you safe, or are you at risk?

    _____

3. If something is imperceptibly approaching you, do you know it's coming?

    _____

4. If an object has been pulverized, is it enhanced or has it most likely become useless?

    _____

5. If a person is melancholy, is that person ready to party or more likely to want to be left alone?

    _____

6. Do your capillary veins carry the bulk of your blood flow?

    _____

7. Give an example of something that is multifaceted.

    _____

8. Would someone be more likely to find expertise in ballistics at the FBI or among one's friends?

    _____

VOCABULARY CROSSWORD
Reading Assignment 1 Fahrenheit 451
Use the word list from Part II Matching

Deflected from a straight path (9)
Fine; small in diameter (9)
Having many faces or sides (12)
Having or revealing little emotion (6)
Impossible to detect by ordinary senses (13)
Reduced to powder (10)
Sadness; gloominess (10)
The study of the dynamics of projectiles (10)

STUDY & DISCUSSION QUESTIONS
Reading Assignment 1 Fahrenheit 451

1. What is Montag's occupation, and how is his job different from what we expect?

2. Of what is the number 451 on Montag's helmet symbolic?

3. What is a "minstrel man," and why does Bradbury choose this image?

4. What words and phrases does Bradbury use to give a feeling of mystery or anticipation just before Montag first meets Clarisse?

5. Why is Clarisse able to "get to" Montag in their first meetings?

Study & Discussion Questions: Fahrenheit 451 Reading Assignment 1, Page 2

6. Explain in what ways Clarisse and Mildred are different from each other.

7. Montag is thinking about Clarisse when he thinks, "...how many people did you know that refracted your own light back at you?" How does this thought apply to Clarisse and Montag?

8. One of the men who comes to pump Mildred's stomach says, "You don't need an M.D., case like this; all you need is two handymen, clean up the problem in half an hour." How does this statement aptly sum up the whole process described in the preceding paragraphs?

9. What does the Hound's reaction to Montag at the firehouse tell us?

10. Early in the first reading assignment, Montag's ventilator grill is mentioned twice. Review these two references and tell what you think is behind the ventilator grill.

Study & Discussion Questions: Fahrenheit 451 Reading Assignment 1, Page 3

11. Clarisse calls herself "crazy" and "a fool." Others call her "anti-social." Do you think Clarisse is crazy, a fool, or anti-social? Support your answer with logical reasoning and examples from the text.

12. About school, Clarisse says, "It's all a lot of funnels and water poured down the spout and out the bottom, and them telling us it's wine when it's not." What does she mean?

13. Beatty asks Montag if he has a guilty conscience. Montag glances up quickly. Then Beatty stares at him and begins to laugh softly. What do you make of this exchange?

14. How is the world Clarisse and Montag live in similar to our world today?

15. Is our world more like the "old days" Clarisse's uncle speaks of, or is it more like the world of Clarisse and Montag's time?

Study & Discussion Questions: Fahrenheit 451 Reading Assignment 1, Page 4

ADDITIONAL PASSAGES FOR DISCUSSION

1. Discuss the imagery in the passage beginning, "The autumn leaves blew over the moonlit pavement...."

2. "You laugh when I haven't been funny and you answer right off. You never stop to think what I've asked you."

3. They walked the rest of the way in silence, hers thoughtful, his a kind of clenching and uncomfortable silence in which he shot her accusing glances.

4. Go on, anyway, shove the bore down, slush up the emptiness, if such a thing could be brought out in the throb of the suction snake.

5. Only an hour, but the world had melted down and sprung up in a new and colorless form.

6. "What a shame," she said. "You're not in love with anyone."

7. He saw the silver needle extend upon the air an inch, pull back, extend, pull back. The growl simmered in the beast and it looked at him.

8. My uncle says his grandfather remembered when children didn't kill each other.

COMIC STRIP CHARACTERS
Fahrenheit 451

The first reading assignment has some great material for making comic-strip-style representations of the characters.

At the opening of the story, there's **Montag**, a larger-than-life fireman holding that python hose spewing venomous kerosene.

Later, a few pages from the end of the reading assignment section, **Beatty and the Mechanical Hound** provide excellent material for a cartoon artist to run with.

And then, there's **Clarisse**...dear, sweet Clarisse with all the images of nature associated with her. You can find 3 different scenes involving Clarisse in this section of the book, from which you can draw on for ideas.

Your assignment is to draw 3 comic strip cells, one for each of the three references above.
- You can make them any size you want, but no smaller than 3 x 3, so details can be included and seen.
- They should be done in color.
- Have fun exaggerating their qualities, as a comic strip artist would!

Here's how to go about doing it:
1. Go back to the text and re-read the parts relating to each character before you begin to draw, to get ideas and mental pictures to work from.
2. Jot down notes about what will be included in your images, notes for each of the three drawings. Consider things like: characters' facial expressions, body stance, other things in the image (like background images, things the character would be holding, etc.), colors that will be used, and size of the images, etc.
3. Look at some comic strip images to see how different artists draw within the individual cells and how they show faces and other elements--angles, perspectives, etc. Choose some cell layouts that you think might work well for your images, and use them as models as you do your own work.
4. Decide on the media you will use (markers, computer, paints) and gather your materials.
5. Make rough-draft sketches showing the layouts of each image.
6. Proceed with creating your masterpieces!

CLARISSE'S POEM (SONG)
Fahrenheit 451

Isn't it a nice time of night to walk? I like to smell things and look at things, and sometimes stay up all night, walking, and watch the sun rise.
--- Clarisse

She isn't physically present in any scenes after the first reading assignment section, yet her presence is felt throughout the novel. Have you ever met someone like that...someone whose personality sticks with you in a positive way long after he or she has left the room...someone like Clarisse?

Your assignment is to write a poem (or lyrics) entitled Clarisse's Poem (or Song), in which you convey the essence of Clarisse's character based on her scenes in the novel.

There is no specific length requirement, but it is highly unlikely you could do this assignment justice in just a few lines.

Here's how to go about doing it:
1. Skim through the text of Reading Assignment 1 to locate and reread the passages in which Clarisse participates.
2. Make notes about the things she does, what she says, how she is described. You can use words or phrases directly from the text.
3. Analyze what you have read and the notes you have made to construct in your own mind the key things that made Clarisse the person she was. What is the essence of her character?
4. Circle, jot down, or note what words or phrases would best convey "Clarisse."
5. Choose a form for your work: If you do a poem, what kind of a poem will you do? Free form? A poem with a strict rhyming pattern? A series of Haiku poems? If you do song lyrics, will they be in the form of rap? To the tune of a particular song you know or like or think would be appropriate for Clarisse?
6. Begin a rough draft of organizing words and phrases into your form. Don't be afraid to add your own words, not just words from the text. This is *your* work; you're not stuck with only Mr. Bradbury's words. Be descriptive. Make your readers *feel* who Clarisse was.
7. Rework, reword, rearrange, edit. Craft your poem (or song) about Clarisse carefully, to be the best you can make it.
8. Then, write a final draft. Decorate your final draft with appropriate illustrations if you are so inclined.

BACK IN THE DAY
Fahrenheit 451

Have you ever found an old coin, maybe dated 30 or 40 years ago, and wondered where all that coin had traveled in all those years...who else had it, what they bought with it? It's fun to imagine where it has been. The sad part is that you can never really *know*; it's not like the thing can tell its life's story.

Old *people*, on the other hand, can. They can tell you where they've been, what they've seen first-hand, what they remember about how things used to be, back in the day...like Clarisse's grandfather.

In terms of the message in Fahrenheit 451, people didn't *know* what had been done in the past; they just assumed that whatever they were being told was the truth. That often is a good assumption...but not always. If you don't know that firemen used to put out fires, and you see that they only start fires now...then it would be easy to assume that they never put out fires, if no one ever told you that they did. Did you know that all gas stations used to be full service and you never had to pump your own gas? The attendant did it--and he washed your windshield and checked your oil, too! ...Or did you just assume that everyone always pumped his or her own gas? A thing like that doesn't make a lot of difference, but some other things *do*.

If we don't talk to our grandfathers and grandmothers, our great-aunts and great-uncles, the old fella who lives down the street, or that old woman in the nursing home, we lose the passing-on of first-hand information. 30 or 40 years from now when your grandchild asks you how something was back in the 1900's, you may not have experienced it, but you can say, "My mother, my grandmother, or that old fella down the street once told me..." And *their* first-hand experience is passed on through several generations. You (thankfully) might never know what it was like to not be able to drink from the same water fountain as another person...but someone else can express to you the humiliation, the anger, the frustration he or she felt. And you know it was real. And because you know it was real, your grandchild will know it was real, too, when you tell her about it.

So *talk* with an old person...frequently. Listen to the stories of his life experiences, ask her about how things were different back in the day. What was it like when he came home from Vietnam? What did it mean to her to see the first man walk on the moon? What things did his grandfather tell *him* about why he came to America? Ask questions, listen, and remember. Then, some day in the future, if the history books say Americans never went to the moon; that's just an old story, you will recognize the lie, you will *know* what really happened.

Your assignment is to talk (and listen) to an old person. If you don't have old relatives, visit the American Legion or a nursing home, explain your assignment, and ask for some time to talk with someone there.

Fahrenheit 451: Back In The Day Activity, page 2

Some things to keep in mind:
- *Speak clearly and be patient.*
- *Be prepared with a list of questions.* If you really listen to what is said and if you think about it rather than just letting it go in one ear and out the other, you will probably also naturally have questions within the conversation.
- *Take notes so you can refer to them later.* If you have a recording device, ask the person you talk with if you may record the conversation rather than taking notes during it. Then go back later to make notes from the recording.
- *Be polite.* You may bump into a topic that the person is uncomfortable talking about. Just go on to something else. Your goal is not to upset anyone. Also, "please" and "thank you" are still appreciated by most people.

Here are some sample questions to get you started:
- What things from your childhood do you remember most vividly?
- What world events have had the most effect on you in your lifetime?
- What was your favorite thing to do when you were my age?
- Did you know your grandparents or great-aunts and uncles, and if so, what do you remember about them? What did they do for a living?
- What's the most important thing you have learned in your lifetime?

Add more of your own questions to this list. The point of the questions is to find out what really happened and what things were really like "back in the day," at a time before you can remember.

After you complete your interview, write a narrative telling about your experience with the interview. Here are some guidelines for this writing assignment:

Write an *introductory paragraph* in which you state the name and age of your interviewee and your relationship to that person. You could also mention how you felt about doing the interview. Were you nervous? Were you looking forward to it? Were you dreading it?

The body of your narrative should tell about the interview itself.
- You could organize the body of the narrative by making a paragraph for each of the questions you asked for which the interviewee had lengthy or interesting answers. Based on the first question above, the topic sentence for the paragraph might be something like this: "The thing [interviewee name] remembers most vividly about [his/her] childhood is...." And then your paragraph would include some of the details from the interviewee's reply.
- Another way to organize the body of the narrative would be by your reactions to the information you received in reply to your questions. For example, "I was surprised to find out that..." or "The most touching moment, for me, in the interview was..." or "It made me sad to find out that..." Think about how you felt about different parts of the interview conversation to come up with your own topic sentences. Then, fill out your paragraphs with details about what was said that made you feel that way, and why.

Write a concluding paragraph stating what you will remember most about this interviewing experience, and why.

WHAT'S IN YOUR WINDOW?
Fahrenheit 451

He stood outside the talking house in the shadows, thinking he might even tap on their door and whisper, "Let me come in. I won't say anything. I just want to listen. What is it you're saying?" --Guy Montag

Guy stood outside of Clarisse's home that evening, listening to the conversation. He wanted to hear more. If Montag were to stand outside your home, looking in your window, what would he see and hear on any typical evening?

Your assignment is to describe from Montag's point of view what he sees and hears while standing outside of your home one evening, looking in your window.

You may write this in any format you choose:
- as a descriptive essay
- as a play scene
- as a poem or song lyrics
- as a comic strip

Here's how to begin:
1. Choose the setting. In what room are things most likely to be going on at your house in the evening?
2. Make some notes describing the room--essential as well as unusual characteristics.
3. Make some notes about who will be in the room.
4. Make notes about what kind of conversation or activity that will typically be going on.
5. Go back and sketch in any dialogue that might be happening
6. Decide on the format for your description.
7. Begin writing a draft.

Think about and be prepared to state what Montag's reaction to what he sees and/or hears might be (and why you think he would feel that way).
- Would he want to come in just to listen?
- Would he be bored?
- Would he want to stay at the window watching?

Copyrighted Materials

READER RESPONSE
Fahrenheit 451

Complete a reader response journal entry for each reading assignment.
Here are some ideas of things you could write about in your entries!

CHECK YOUR UNDERSTANDING
Explain how the story is making sense to you.
Give examples & note page numbers.
Explain the setting, mood, point of view, conflicts, or character relationships.
Discuss the stated themes.

MAKE INFERENCES
Explain your thoughts about the feelings or motives of the characters.
Discuss implied themes.

MAKE AND REVISE PREDICTIONS
At the end of each assignment, make a prediction about what you think will happen next.
After you read, go back and check your predictions.
Tell if you had to revise them, and why.

ASK QUESTIONS
Ask questions about scenes or events that are confusing.
Record the answers when you discuss the questions in class or if you later find the answer in the story.

GIVE YOUR OPINION
Give your opinion about the literary quality of the work.
Discuss the author's style, use of language, and use of literary devices.
Tell why you do or do not like the story or a character.
Compare the book with others you have read.

MAKE CONNECTIONS
Think about ways the characters and events relate to your own life experiences. Put yourself in a character's place and discuss how you would feel or what you would do in that situation.

READER RESPONSE: Reading Assignment 1
Fahrenheit 451

Use this page to write down your reader response entry. Try to write a whole page of content.

General Topic _____

_____
_____
_____
_____
_____
_____
_____
_____
_____
_____
_____
_____
_____
_____
_____
_____
_____
_____
_____
_____
_____
_____
_____

A Few Ideas (Pick one or create your own.)
- How would you have felt if you were Montag and came home to find Mildred in that condition?
- Do you think you would like to have Clarisse as a good friend? Why or why not?
- Clarisse gives her opinion of school. Do you agree with her? What's your opinion of school?
- Do you know people who just give automatic responses without thinking? How's it make you feel when you talk with them?

NOTES
Fahrenheit 451

READING ASSIGNMENT 2
Fahrenheit 451

THIS ASSIGNMENT COVERS APPROXIMATELY
THE LAST HALF OF CHAPTER ONE:
"THE HEARTH AND THE SALAMANDER"

START:
"The flutter of cards, motion of hands, of eyelids, the drone of the time-voice in the firehouse ceiling '. . . one thirty-five, Thursday morning, November 4th, . . . one thirty-six . . . one thirty-seven A.M. . . .'"

END:
End of chapter one

NOTES
Fahrenheit 451

CHARACTER NOTES
Reading Assignment 2 Fahrenheit 451

As you read Assignment 2 use this graphic organizer to jot down information about characters.

MONTAG	BEATTY

WOMAN WITH BOOKS	MILDRED

EVENTS & POINTS OF INTEREST
Reading Assignment 2 Fahrenheit 451

As you read Assignment 2 make notes of the series of main events that take place. Put them in the order that they are given in the text.

_____

_____

_____

_____

_____

_____

_____

OTHER POINTS OF INTEREST TO IDENTIFY OR KNOW THE SIGNIFICANCE OF:

The ventilator grill

An ordinary kitchen match

Montag's sickness

The beetle

Montag's books

VOCABULARY WORK FOR ASSIGNMENT 2
Fahrenheit 451

PART I: Using Prior Knowledge And Contextual Clues
Use any clues you can find in the sentences from the text combined with your prior knowledge and write what you think the bold word means.

1. . . . all the sounds came to Montag, behind the barrier he had momentarily **erected**.

   _____

2. Were all firemen picked then for their looks as well as their **proclivities**?

   _____

3. Beatty, Stoneman, and Black ran up the sidewalk, suddenly **odious** and fat in their plump fireproof slickers.

   _____

4. He felt one hand and then the other work his coat free and let it slump to the floor. . . . His hands were **ravenous**. And his eyes were beginning to feel hunger, as if they must look at something, anything, everything.

   _____

5. "Life becomes one big **pratfall**, Montag; everything bang, boff, and wow!"

   _____

6. There was no **dictum**, no declaration, no censorship, to start with, no!

   _____

7. Cram them full of **noncombustible** data, chock them so damned full of 'facts' they feel stuffed, but absolutely 'brilliant' with information.

   _____

8. I'll think I'm responding to the play, when it's only a **tactile** reaction to vibration.

   _____

Vocabulary Work For Fahrenheit 451 Assignment 2, Page 2

PART II: Matching
Considering the usage in Part I, match the vocabulary words to their definitions.

_____ 1. erected   A. Humiliating failure; a fall on the buttocks

_____ 2. proclivities   B. Predispositions; tendencies

_____ 3. odious   C. Does not burn easily

_____ 4. ravenous   D. Arousing strong dislike or displeasure

_____ 5. pratfall   E. Extremely hungry; greedy for gratification

_____ 6. dictum   F. Authoritative pronouncement

_____ 7. noncombustible   G. Relating to the sense of touch

_____ 8. tactile   H. Set up; established

Part III: Cloze Passage
Fill in the blanks with the appropriate vocabulary words from the list above.

The scaffolding had been _____ by _____ of the patron who wished to paint the ceiling of his ancestral home. The project required a complete, _____, hands-on approach as the task was rather _____ due to the fact the ceiling was 100 feet high. The artist was _____ to finish, especially considering his _____ towards acrophobia. On the very first day he had a humiliating _____ sending him with a lamp in his hand into a bucket of chemicals. Fortunately they were _____.

Vocabulary Work For Fahrenheit 451 Assignment 2, Page 3

PART IV: Words In Practice
Answer the questions and be able to give short explanations to justify your answers.

1. When you erect a monument, do you build it up or tear it down?
   _____

2. Name something that would be a good proclivity.
   _____

3. If you are asked to do something you think is odious, are you happy to do it or would you rather not?
   _____

4. Who is someone who would be ravenous?
   _____

5. Give an example of a pratfall.
   _____

6. Who would create a dictum?
   _____

7. Which is noncombustible, a match or an asbestos tile?
   _____

8. What is something that is pleasant to the tactile senses?
   _____

VOCABULARY CROSSWORD
Reading Assignment 2 Fahrenheit 451
Use the word list from Part II Matching

Arousing strong dislike or displeasure (6)
Authoritative pronouncement (6)
Does not burn easily (14)
Extremely hungry; greedy for gratification (8)
Humiliating failure; a fall on the buttocks (8)
Predispositions; tendencies (12)
Relating to the sense of touch (7)
Set up; established (7)

STUDY & DISCUSSION QUESTIONS
Reading Assignment 2 Fahrenheit 451

1. When he goes to the firehouse, Montag realizes that all firemen look alike, and he wonders if they were chosen simply because they look that way. If that is true, what does it say about the society in which they live?

2. Early in the second reading assignment, Beatty states, "Any man's insane who thinks he can fool the government and us." Do you agree or disagree with that statement? Support your viewpoint.

3. When the firemen respond to the alarm at North Elm, the woman is still there. How does her presence "spoil the ritual" for the firemen?

4. Before the firemen burn her books, the woman says, "Play the man, Master Ridley; we shall this day light such a candle, by God's grace, in England, as I trust shall never be put out." Explain the significance of this quotation.

5. When Montag returns home after burning the woman's home, he describes his hands as "infected." What does he mean by this?

Study & Discussion Questions: Fahrenheit 451 Reading Assignment 2, Page 2

6. How does Millie break the news of Clarisse's death to Montag? Why is it important that she does it in that way?

7. What do you think Montag means when he says, "But that was another Mildred...so deep inside this one, and so bothered, really bothered, that the two women had never met." ?

8. Beatty says, "We must all be alike. Not everyone born free and equal, but everyone made equal. Each man the image of every other; then all are happy, for there are no mountains to make them cower, to judge themselves against." Do you agree with Beatty's vision of happiness? Why or why not?

9. In his speech, Beatty describes their world as being happy. Do you think he believes it? Support your answer with quotes from the text.

Study & Discussion Questions: Fahrenheit 451 Reading Assignment 2, Page 3

10. Why doesn't Mildred tell Beatty about the book she finds?

11. Toward the end of Part One, Montag wonders why the firemen were so afraid of people like Clarisse. Why do you think they might be?

12. Summarize Beatty's explanation of how and why society changed in the 20th Century.

Study & Discussion Questions: Fahrenheit 451 Reading Assignment 2, Page 4

ADDITIONAL PASSAGES FOR DISCUSSION

1. Discuss the imagery used in the paragraph beginning, "Books bombarded his shoulders..." (pg. 34 of the 60th Anniversary edition).

2. "Will you turn the parlor off?"
   "That's my family."

3. "We burned a thousand books. We burned a woman."
   "Well?"

4. "...this fire'll last me the rest of my life. God! I've been trying to put it out, in my mind, all night..."
   "You should have thought of that before becoming a fireman."

5. "We need not to be let alone. We need to be really bothered once in a while."

6. This time, Mildred ran. The yammering voices stopped yelling in the parlor.

7. "You ask Why to a lot of things and you wind up very unhappy indeed, if you keep at it. The poor girl's better off dead."

PLAY THE MAN, MASTER RIDLEY
Fahrenheit 451

The woman on North Elm decided she would rather die than live without her books. Perhaps she also had heard that people with books were sometimes sent to the insane asylum. At some point, though, she made up her mind to deliberately stay in her burning home with her burning books. No doubt she had thought about this before the alarm was ever called in. When you break the law, you usually think about the consequences and what you would do if you got caught.

We're going to diverge from the actual story of Fahrenheit 451 for a little bit. Suppose the North Elm woman knew ahead of time that the alarm was going to be called in, and she had already decided to go down with her books. After making this decision, she wrote a letter to her daughter, which she mailed when she found out the alarm had been called in. What would she have said to her daughter in that letter?

Your assignment is to write a letter from the North Elm woman to her daughter (or son, your choice) explaining why she refused to leave her home, and giving her daughter (or son) her parting words.

- Be thorough in your explanations
- Use a friendly letter format

Here's a way to go about doing this assignment:
1. Pretend you are the North Elm woman.
2. Think about why you would do what she did, knowing what you know about her world. Jot down any reasons you can think of as to why she would choose to do this.
3. Think about what you would say to your child, knowing you would soon be gone. What words of advice, what final words would you say? Jot down any ideas you have.
4. Look over your notes. Choose the best reasons and advice. Organize them in a logical way. Do any thoughts go together or naturally flow from one to another? Identify those kinds of things in your notes.
5. Write a rough draft of your letter. A few words of introduction, stating your intentions, would be appropriate. Follow that with your reasons. Follow that with any advice or final words you have.
6. Re-read, revise, have someone else read your letter and make suggestions. Edit and revise as necessary until you are happy with the final draft.

BOOKS, BOOKS, BOOKS
Fahrenheit 451

Find 10 different kinds of reading materials in your library or media center. Tell what kind each is, list the tiles, read the covers to see what they are about and fill in the About column, and then tell if each looks interesting to you or not. A few boxes are bigger in case you need more room for some titles

Kind	Title	About	Interesting To You?

KWL Reading Assignment 2
Fahrenheit 451

Write what you know and what you want to find out.
After you have read the next section, fill in what you learned.

K What I Know	**W** What I Want To Find Out	**L** What I Learned

READER RESPONSE: Reading Assignment 2
Fahrenheit 451

Use this page to write down your reader response entry. Try to write a whole page of content.

General Topic _____

_____
_____
_____
_____
_____
_____
_____
_____
_____
_____
_____
_____
_____
_____
_____
_____
_____
_____
_____
_____
_____
_____

A Few Ideas (Pick one or create your own.)
- What do you think of the woman who lit the match to set her home and herself on fire? Is there anything you would be willing to do that for?
- If books were being banned, which books would you stash copies of? Tell why for each.
- Beatty talks about how society changed in the 20th century. In what kind of a society would you like to live? Tell a few main characteristics of it and say why those are important to you.
- Did you think Beatty would find out about the book under Montag's pillow? What would have been going through your mind if you were Montag?

READING ASSIGNMENT 3
Fahrenheit 451

THIS ASSIGNMENT COVERS
ALL OF CHAPTER TWO
"THE SAND AND THE SIEVE"

START:
Beginning of chapter two

END:
End of chapter two

NOTES
Fahrenheit 451

CHARACTER NOTES
Reading Assignment 3 Fahrenheit 451

As you read Assignment 3 use this graphic organizer to jot down information about characters.

MONTAG

FABER

MILDRED

BEATTY

MRS. PHELPS

EVENTS & POINTS OF INTEREST
Reading Assignment 3 Fahrenheit 451

As you read Assignment 3 make notes of the series of main events that take place. Put them in the order that they are given in the text.

_____

_____

_____

_____

_____

_____

_____

OTHER POINTS OF INTEREST TO IDENTIFY OR KNOW THE SIGNIFICANCE OF:

The White Clown

The sieve and the sand

Denham's dental detergent

3 things that are missing

The green bullet

The Sea Of Faith

VOCABULARY WORK FOR ASSIGNMENT 3
Fahrenheit 451

PART I: Using Prior Knowledge And Contextual Clues

Use any clues you can find in the sentences from the text combined with your prior knowledge and write what you think the bold word means.

1. ...he talked in a **cadenced** voice...and when an hour had passed he said something to Montag and Montag sensed it was a rhymeless poem.

   _____

2. The train radio vomited upon Montag, in **retaliation**, a great tonload of music made of tin, copper, silver, chromium and brass.

   _____

3. Books were only one type of **receptacle** where we stored a lot of things we were afraid we might forget.

   _____

4. Proof of my terrible **cowardice**.

   _____

5. On one wall a woman smiled and drank orange juice **simultaneously**. How does she do both at once, thought Montag...

   _____

6. For these were the hands that had acted on their own, no part of him, here was where the conscience first **manifested** itself to snatch books, dart off with Job and Ruth and Willie Shakespeare, and now, in the firehouse, these hands seemed gloved with blood.

   _____

7. You towered with rage, yelled quotes at me, I calmly **parried** every thrust. Power, I said.

   _____

8. The folly of mistaking a metaphor for a proof, a torrent of **verbiage** for a spring of capital truths, and oneself as an oracle, is inborn in us, Mr. Valery once said.

   _____

Vocabulary Work For Fahrenheit 451 Assignment 3, Page 2

PART II: Matching
Considering the usage in Part I, match the vocabulary words to their definitions.

_____ 1. cadenced   A. Ignoble fear in the face of danger

_____ 2. retaliation   B. A container that holds matter

_____ 3. receptacle   C. At the same time

_____ 4. cowardice   D. Returning like for like

_____ 5. simultaneously   E. Wordiness

_____ 6. manifested   F. Showed; revealed

_____ 7. parried   G. Deflected; avoided

_____ 8. verbiage   H. With a rhythmic flow

Part III: Cloze Passage
Fill in the blanks with the appropriate vocabulary words from the list above.

The newscaster began his report with a _____ voice which _____ a _____ of unparalleled intensity. _____ was his motive, for he was accusing another station of _____ because of the underhanded way they were attacking his broadcasts. He had previously _____ their attacks, but now he was _____ responding to them openly and hitting back with his own assertions about their station. At the end of his broadcast, he threw his notes into a trash _____ to close with a dramatic flourish.

Vocabulary Work For Fahrenheit 451 Assignment 3, Page 3

PART IV: Words In Practice
Answer the questions and be able to give short explanations to justify your answers.

1. Does a cadenced march help keep soldiers in step together or make being in step difficult?
_____

2. If someone came up and slapped you in the face, is it likely you would want to retaliate?
_____

3. What is one common household receptacle?
_____

4. Is cowardice on the battlefield usually considered to be heroic?
_____

5. Name two things that often happen simultaneously.
_____

6. In what ways does the flu manifest itself?
_____

7. In what occupation is a lot of verbiage required?
_____

8. What is something that can be parried?
_____

VOCABULARY CROSSWORD
Reading Assignment 3 Fahrenheit 451
Use the word list from Part II Matching

A container that holds matter (10)
Deflected; avoided (7)
Happening at the same time (14)
Ignoble fear in the face of danger (9)
Returning like for like, especially evil (11)
Showed; revealed (10)
With a rhythmic flow (8)
Wordiness (8)

STUDY & DISCUSSION QUESTIONS
Reading Assignment 3 Fahrenheit 451

1. How do we know that the dog at the door is the mechanical hound?

2. Why is the event with the mechanical hound at the door significant?

3. The details in this book are important. There are only a few sentences about the door-voice in the incident with the dog at the door, but they are important:
    "Someone--the door--why doesn't the door-voice tell us---"
    "I shut it off."
   What do we learn about Montag and Mildred from these two lines?

4. Why does Montag insist on continuing to read the books?

5. From Mildred's point of view, explain why the parlor walls are better than books.

Study & Discussion Questions: Fahrenheit 451 Reading Assignment 3, Page 2

6. Mildred asks Montag, "Why should I read? What *for*?" Summarize Montag's answer by finishing his sentence, "An hour a day, two hours, with these books, and maybe . . ."

7. Compare and contrast Montag's first meeting with Faber in the park with his first meeting with Clarisse.

8. Montag asks Millie "Does the White Clown love you . . . does your 'family' love you?" What is the significance of Montag's questions?

9. What is the difference between talking "things" and talking "the meaning of things"?

10. "The train radio vomited upon Montag, in retaliation, a great tonload of music made of tin, copper, silver, chromium, and brass." What type of figure of speech is exemplified in this sentence? The music is in retaliation of what? Why is the music described as being made of metals?

Study & Discussion Questions: Fahrenheit 451 Reading Assignment 3, Page 3

11. Faber says that there are three things missing from the world. What are they?

12. Faber calls himself a coward for not speaking up against the bad changes in their society as they were happening, before it was too late. He later calls Montag "brave" after he learns that Montag stole the Bible. Do you think Faber is/was a coward and Montag is brave, or do you think their actions could be governed by something other than cowardice and/or bravery?

13. Montag and Faber hatch a plan to plant books in Firemen's houses to help bring down the system, while also setting up clandestine reading rooms. Do you think this is a good plan? Evaluate their chances for success.

14. Why are Millie and her friends made so nervous when Montag turns the TV walls off?

15. Describe Mrs. Bowles's parenting style and describe the type of children she is raising.

Study & Discussion Questions: Fahrenheit 451 Reading Assignment 3, Page 4

16. Compare Mrs. Phelps's responses and reactions to Montag with Montag's responses and reactions to Clarisse.

17. Earlier in the book, Beatty says "If you don't want a man unhappy politically, don't give him two sides of a question to worry him; give him one. Better yet, give him none." On what criteria do Millie and her friends judge the political candidates, and how does their political conversation between Millie and her friends relate to Beatty's statement?

18. Why does Mrs. Phelps start crying in response to the poem?

19. Chapter Two is entitled "The Sieve and the Sand." To what does this refer?

Study & Discussion Questions: Fahrenheit 451 Reading Assignment 3, Page 5

ADDITIONAL PASSAGES FOR DISCUSSION

1. Faber tells Montag "It's not the books you need, it's some of the things that once were in books. The same things could be in the 'parlor families' today." What do you think he means by this?

2. "We are living in a time when flowers are trying to live on flowers, instead of growing on good rain and black loam."

3. "We cannot tell the precise moment when friendship is formed. As in filling a vessel drop by drop, there is at last a drop which makes it run over; so in a series of kindnesses there is at least one which makes the heart run over."

4. Mildred kicked the book. "Books aren't people. You read and I look all around, but there isn't *anybody*!...my 'family' is people. They tell me things; *I* laugh, *they* laugh! and the colors!"

5. "Who's more important, me or that Bible?" She was beginning to shriek now, sitting there like a wax doll melting in its own heat."

6. "My wife's dying. A friend of mine's already dead. Someone who may have been a friend was burnt less than twenty-four hours ago. You're the only one I knew might help me. To see. To see . . ."

7. "Nobody listens anymore. I can't talk to the walls because they're yelling at *me*. I can't talk to my wife; she listens to the *walls*. I just want someone to hear what I have to say. And maybe if I talk long enough, it'll make sense. And I want you to teach me to understand what I read."

8. "And don't look to be saved in any *one* thing, person, machine, or library. Do your own bit of saving, and if you drown, at least die knowing you were headed for shore."

9. "Remember, the firemen are rarely necessary. The public itself stopped reading of its own accord. . . . People are having *fun*."

Study & Discussion Questions: Fahrenheit 451 Reading Assignment 3, Page 6

Additional Passages For Discussion, Continued

10. I remember the newspapers dying like huge moths. No one wanted them back. No one missed them. And then the Government, seeing how advantageous it was to have people reading only about passionate lips and the fist in the stomach, circled the situation with your fire-eaters."

11. "I don't want to change sides and just be *told* what to do. There's no reason to change if I do that."

12. "He is no wise man who will quit a certainty for an uncertainty."

13. "But remember the Captain belongs to the most dangerous enemy to truth and freedom, the solid unmoving cattle of the majority."

14. The men ran like cripples in their clumsy boots, as quietly as spiders.

DOVER BEACH
Fahrenheit 451

Dover Beach
BY MATTHEW ARNOLD

The sea is calm tonight.
The tide is full, the moon lies fair
Upon the straits; on the French coast the light
Gleams and is gone; the cliffs of England stand,
Glimmering and vast, out in the tranquil bay.
Come to the window, sweet is the night-air!
Only, from the long line of spray
Where the sea meets the moon-blanched land,
Listen! you hear the grating roar
Of pebbles which the waves draw back, and fling,
At their return, up the high strand,
Begin, and cease, and then again begin,
With tremulous cadence slow, and bring
The eternal note of sadness in.

Sophocles long ago
Heard it on the Ægean, and it brought
Into his mind the turbid ebb and flow
Of human misery; we
Find also in the sound a thought,
Hearing it by this distant northern sea.

The Sea of Faith
Was once, too, at the full, and round earth's shore
Lay like the folds of a bright girdle furled.
But now I only hear
Its melancholy, long, withdrawing roar,
Retreating, to the breath
Of the night-wind, down the vast edges drear
And naked shingles of the world.

Ah, love, let us be true
To one another! for the world, which seems
To lie before us like a land of dreams,
So various, so beautiful, so new,
Hath really neither joy, nor love, nor light,
Nor certitude, nor peace, nor help for pain;
And we are here as on a darkling plain
Swept with confused alarms of struggle and flight,
Where ignorant armies clash by night.

Notes:

tranquil = peaceful; calm

tremulous = trembling
cadence = rhythmic pace

Aegean = the Aegean Sea, part of the Mediterranean Sea
turbid = muddy; cloudy; not clear

The sound of the sea waves reminded Sophocles of the coming and going of good and bad times for humankind.

---

girdle = something that encircles or confines
furled = rolled tightly in upon itself

At one time, humankind had faith, but people no longer do.

---

certitude = certainty

Without faith, there is no certainty or peace in the world. All we have left is each other, so let's be true to one another in a confused world full of war.

TV FAVORITES
Fahrenheit 451

List your three most favorite television shows below.

1. _____
2. _____
3. _____

For each of the TV shows you listed, answer these questions:
What kind of a show is it (reality, sports, news, drama...)?

1. _____ 2. _____ 3. _____

What is the level of intellectual engagement or educational value of the show (on a scale of 1 to 10 with 10 being the highest level of intellectual engagement or educational value)?

1. _____ 2. _____ 3. _____

What values does the show promote?

1. _____
2. _____
3. _____

What kind of language is used on the show (common, vulgar, intellectual)?

1. _____ 2. _____ 3. _____

Is the show purely "entertainment," or does it have other value (if so, what)?

1. _____ 2. _____ 3. _____

Would it fit well into programming on the Parlor Walls (yes or no)?
1. _____ 2. _____ 3. _____

Has this program become your "family"? Do you schedule your activities around seeing it and talk a lot about it?

1. _____ 2. _____ 3. _____

Why do you like this show so much? What about it appeals to you?

1. _____
2. _____
3. _____

JUDGING A CANDIDATE
Fahrenheit 451

In Reading Assignment 3, Millie urges her friends to have a discussion about politics to please Guy. Review that section of the text and answer the following questions:

1. On what kinds of things do the women compare and contrast the candidates?

2. On what kinds of things should they compare and contrast the candidates?

3. Do you listen to what the candidates say? Why or why not?

4. What could happen if people would stop listening to what candidates say and would vote based on the criteria the women in the novel use?

5. Does what the candidates say always match up with the actions they take? Explain.

6. Why is it important to both listen to AND evaluate actions of a candidate?

7. Does the moral character of a candidate make a difference? Why or why not?

KWL Reading Assignment 3
Fahrenheit 451

Write what you know and what you want to find out.

After you have read the next section, fill in what you learned.

K What I Know	**W** What I Want To Find Out	**L** What I Learned

READER RESPONSE: Reading Assignment 3
Fahrenheit 451

Use this page to write down your reader response entry. Try to write a whole page of content.

General Topic _____

_____
_____
_____
_____
_____
_____
_____
_____
_____
_____
_____
_____
_____
_____
_____
_____
_____
_____
_____
_____
_____
_____
_____

A Few Ideas (Pick one or create your own.)
- What do you think of the parlor walls? Do you think having them would be awesome or terrible? Why?
- Do you like to have quiet time to think, or not? How do you feel about silence?
- Would your parenting style be like Mrs. Bowles's, or would you want to be with your children? Explain why.
- Has a poem, story, song, or movie touched you and made you cry? What about it made you have such strong feelings?

NOTES
Fahrenheit 451

READING ASSIGNMENT 4
Fahrenheit 451

THIS ASSIGNMENT COVERS
ALL OF CHAPTER THREE
"BURNING BRIGHT"

START:
Beginning Of Chapter Three

END:
End Of Chapter Three

NOTES
Fahrenheit 451

CHARACTER NOTES
Reading Assignment 4 Fahrenheit 451

As you read Assignment 4 use this graphic organizer to jot down information about characters.

MONTAG	BEATTY

FABER	MILDRED
	GRANGER

EVENTS & POINTS OF INTEREST
Reading Assignment 4 Fahrenheit 451

As you read Assignment 4 make notes of the series of main events that take place. Put them in the order that they are given in the text.

_____

_____

_____

_____

_____

_____

_____

OTHER POINTS OF INTEREST TO IDENTIFY OR KNOW THE SIGNIFICANCE OF:

The river

The railroad tracks

The Book of Ecclesiastes

Phoenix

VOCABULARY WORK FOR ASSIGNMENT 4
Fahrenheit 451

PART I: Using Prior Knowledge And Contextual Clues
Use any clues you can find in the sentences from the text combined with your prior knowledge and write what you think the bold word means.

1. The other firemen waited behind him, in the darkness, their faces illumined faintly by the **smoldering** foundation.

   _____

2. The other was like a chunk of burnt pinelog he was carrying along as penance for some **obscure** sin.

   _____

3. Two dozen of them flurried, wavering, **indecisive**, three miles off.

   _____

4. And there on the small screen was the burnt house, and the crowd and something with a sheet over it and out of the sky, fluttering, came the helicopter like a **grotesque** flower.

   _____

5. ...Montag might...see himself dramatized, described, made over, standing there, **limned** in the bright small television screen from outside....

   _____

6. He saw a great **juggernaut** of stars form in the sky and threaten to roll over and crush him.

   _____

7. He smelled the heavy musk like perfume mingled with blood and the gummed exhalation of the animal's breath, all **cardamon** and moss and ragweed odor in this huge night where the trees ran at him....

   _____

8. The most important single thing we had to pound into ourselves is that we were not important; we mustn't be **pedants**; we were not to feel superior to anyone else in the world.

   _____

9. There was a silly damn bird called a Phoenix back before Christ; every few hundred years he built a **pyre** and burned himself up.

   _____

Vocabulary Work For Fahrenheit 451 Assignment 4, Page 2

PART II: Matching
Considering the usage in Part I, match the vocabulary words to their definitions.

_____ 1. smoldering   A. Described; portrayed; delineated

_____ 2. obscure   B. Not able to make a decision

_____ 3. indecisive   C. A pile of combustible materials for burning a corpse

_____ 4. grotesque   D. Bizarre; distorted

_____ 5. limned   E. Burning with little smoke and no flame

_____ 6. juggernaut   F. Overwhelmingly advancing sight crushing all in its path

_____ 7. cardamon   G. Those who flaunt their knowledge

_____ 8. pedants   H. Not clear; partially hidden; remote

_____ 9. pyre   I. An Indian spice

Part III: Cloze Passage
Fill in the blanks with the appropriate vocabulary words from the list above.

The _____ predicted that a meteor would fall. An object initially appeared _____ in the sky, but suddenly the full _____ approached no longer leaving the skeptics _____ about the forecasted event. The rather _____ presence of this phenomenon in the night sky was now before them. When it hit, the meteor created a _____ crater that gave off smells of sulphur and a faint hint of _____, as it had landed in a field where this spice was grown. Depending on the conditions _____ in his insurance policy, the farmer might get reimbursed for the loss of his crops, but probably not for the cow that dropped dead at the shock of the event. The farmer would have to make a _____ and dispose of the poor animal.

Vocabulary Work For Fahrenheit 451 Assignment 4, Page 3

PART IV: Words In Practice
Answer the questions and be able to give short explanations to justify your answers.

1. Would a smoldering fire keep you very warm on a cold winter's night?

_____

2. Name an obscure person in the field of sports, music, or movies.

_____

3. In what occupation would it be bad to be indecisive?

_____

4. At what holiday might you wear something grotesque?

_____

5. What kind of a document might have conditions limned in its pages?

_____

6. Is a juggernaut something to embrace or run from?

_____

7. Would cardamon be more likely to be used by a chef or a mechanic?

_____

8. What characteristics would someone who is a pedant have?

_____

9. What foreign people from long ago are known for funeral pyres?

_____

VOCABULARY CROSSWORD
Reading Assignment 4 Fahrenheit 451
Use the word list from Part II Matching

A pile of combustible materials for burning a corpse (4)
Bizarre; distorted (9)
Burning with little smoke and no flame (10)
Described (6)
Italian herb (8)
Not able to make a decision (10)
Not readily noticed or seen; not commonly known (7)
Overwhelming, advancing sight crushing all in its path (10)
Those who flaunt their knowledge (7)

STUDY & DISCUSSION QUESTIONS
Reading Assignment 4 Fahrenheit 451

1. Beatty confesses that he sent the Hound to Montag's home. Why did he send it?

2. Compare the Mildred we saw at the beginning of the book with the Mildred who flees the house and zooms off in a beetle.

3. What is the significance of the vacuum that occurs when Montag destroys the TV walls?

4. What motivates Montag to pull the trigger on the flame-thrower and set Beatty on fire?

5. Montag believes Beatty wanted to die. Explain why you agree or disagree with him.

6. Montag wonders if the teenagers who almost ran him over just for fun were the ones who ran over Clarisse. Is there any evidence to support this thought? Based on evidence in the book, would you say Clarisse's death was likely a random or a premeditated act?

7. Is what Montag does to Mrs. Black's house a just thing to do? Is it moral? Is it right? Explain why or why not.

8. Explain the symbolism of the things that Montag does in the river.

Study & Discussion Questions: Fahrenheit 451 Reading Assignment 4, Page 2

9. How is the fire in the countryside different from the fire Montag has experienced?

10. Montag listens to the silence and wonders how Millie would take it. What do you think Millie would do if she were with Montag? Do you think she could adapt?

11. Why does the search team find someone else to kill in place of Montag?

12. The men in the countryside have a plan for saving books. What is it, and do you think it is a good plan?

13. Explain Granger's metaphor of the Phoenix.

14. Explain why Granger misses his grandfather but Montag won't miss Millie.

15. Why did Ray Bradbury make Montag the Book of Ecclesiastes rather than some other book?

Study & Discussion Questions: Fahrenheit 451 Reading Assignment 4, Page 3

ADDITIONAL PASSAGES FOR DISCUSSION

1. "By the time the consequences catch up with you, it's too late, isn't it, Montag?"

2. "Now, Montag, you're a burden. And fire will lift you off of my shoulders, clean, quick, sure; nothing to rot later. Antibiotic, aesthetic, practical."

3. Beatty . . . twisted in on himself like a charred wax doll and lay silent.

4. [Montag] stood and he had only one leg. The other was like a chunk of burnt pine log he was carrying along as a penance for some obscure sin.

5. . . . simply a number of children out for a long night of roaring five or six hundred miles in a few moonlit hours, their faces icy with wind, and coming home or not coming at dawn, alive or not alive, that made the adventure.

6. They would have killed me, thought Montag. . . . For no reason at all in the world they would have killed me.

7. Mrs. Black, are you asleep in there? . . . The house did not reply.

8. He felt as if he had left a stage behind and many actors. He felt as if he had left the great seance and all the murmuring ghosts. He was moving from an unreality that was frightening into a reality that was unreal because it was new.

9. . . . the river was mild and leisurely, going away from the people who ate shadows for breakfast and steam for lunch and vapors for supper.

10. This was all he wanted now. Some sign that the immense world would accept him and give him the long time he needed to think all the things that must be thought.

Study & Discussion Questions: Fahrenheit 451 Reading Assignment 4, Page 4

Additional Passages For Discussion, Continued

11. Ane he was surprised to learn how certain he suddenly was of a single fact he could not prove. Once, long ago, Clarisse had walked here, where he was walking now."

12. . . . there was a foolish and yet delicious sense of knowing himself as an animal come from the forest, drawn by the fire.

13. But you can't *make* people listen. They have to come round in their own time, wondering what happened and why the world blew up under them.

14. ". . . shake the tree and knock the great sloth down on his ass."

15. Silently, Granger arose, felt of his arms and legs, swearing, swearing incessantly under his breath, tears dripping from his face.

16. In the trees, the birds that had flown away quickly now came back and settled down.

ECCLESIASTES
Fahrenheit 451

Montag "became" the Book of Ecclesiastes (from the Bible). Below is a passage from the beginning of the Book of Ecclesiastes (New International Version).

Your assignment is to read this passage and (in writing) respond to, discuss, or explain any one of the numbered verses.
- Several paragraphs would be an appropriate length for your written work.

3 What do people gain from all their labors
   at which they toil under the sun?
4 Generations come and generations go,
   but the earth remains forever.
5 The sun rises and the sun sets,
   and hurries back to where it rises.
6 The wind blows to the south
   and turns to the north;
   round and round it goes,
   ever returning on its course.
7 All streams flow into the sea,
   yet the sea is never full.
   To the place the streams come from,
   there they return again.
8 All things are wearisome,
   more than one can say.
   The eye never has enough of seeing,
   nor the ear its fill of hearing.
9 What has been will be again,
   what has been done will be done again;
   there is nothing new under the sun.
10 Is there anything of which one can say,
   "Look! This is something new"?
   It was here already, long ago;
   it was here before our time.
11 No one remembers the former generations,
   and even those yet to come
   will not be remembered
   by those who follow them.

One way to begin the writing portion of the assignment is to re-read each verse and see what ideas come to your mind. When you find one for which you have several ideas, focus on that one. Jot down your ideas. Expand upon them with additional notes. Begin to formulate them into complete thoughts and organize them so one idea will flow to the next. Use examples to help support and explain your statements.

KWL Reading Assignment 4
Fahrenheit 451

Write what you know and what you want to find out.

After you have read the next section, fill in what you learned.

K What I Know	W What I Want To Find Out	L What I Learned

READER RESPONSE: Reading Assignment 4
Fahrenheit 451

Use this page to write down your reader response entry. Try to write a whole page of content.

General Topic _____

_____
_____
_____
_____
_____
_____
_____
_____
_____
_____
_____
_____
_____
_____
_____
_____
_____
_____
_____
_____
_____
_____
_____
_____
_____

A Few Ideas (Pick one or create your own.)
- Would you prosecute Montag for killing Beatty? Why or why not?
- If you could "be" a book (like Montag is Ecclesiastes) what book would you be?
- Is there someone you miss like Granger misses his grandfather? Who? Why?
- Do you like being outdoors in nature? Camping, walking, looking at the stars at night? What?
- How likely do you think it is that a city you know will be destroyed like the city in the book?

NOTES
Fahrenheit 451

WRITING ASSIGNMENTS
Fahrenheit 451

WRITING ASSIGNMENT 1   DUE _____

WRITING ASSIGNMENT 2   DUE _____

WRITING ASSIGNMENT 3   DUE _____

Completed writing assignments can be stapled to the backs of the assignment pages.

NOTES
Fahrenheit 451

WRITING ASSIGNMENT 1
Fahrenheit 451
Fire Escape Plan

PROMPT

Fire has long been a fascinating thing for mankind. It can be useful; it can be pretty; it can keep us warm, but it can also be very dangerous. Every kid knows Smokey the Bear and has been advised how dangerous fire is to our wildlife friends. Everyone knows and fears the possibility of having a house fire while we are snuggled up in our beds at night. We are fortunate that modern technology has brought us sprinkling systems and fire alarms for our homes. The question then becomes, "What do we do when the smoke alarm goes off?"

Your assignment is to make and write down a fire escape plan for your family and your house. You must give written directions as well as make a map for occupants of each bedroom in your home.

PREWRITING
- First of all, draw a little diagram of your house or apartment. It doesn't have to be perfect for this prewriting exercise. Locate the main rooms of your home. Think for a minute. Where would a fire be most likely to start? Probably in the kitchen, near a heating source, or near an area with a lot of electrical wiring. Locate these and any other areas in your home that are areas where a fire might be likely to start. Put an X on each of those areas.
- Where are the bedrooms in your home in relation to the X marks? Find the best route of escape for the occupants of each of the bedrooms. Mark them on your diagram. If the X marks eliminate all routes of escape, deal with the X marks that are most likely to be trouble spots.
- Think for a minute and make a list of the things that will need to be done to get everyone out safely. Next to each job, write down the name of the person who should be responsible for that job.

DRAFTING
- Write an introductory paragraph telling the circumstances of the prospective fire.
- Write one paragraph for each member of your family, giving them simple, specific instructions as to what to do if there is a fire in your home while you are all in bed asleep. Each person should start from his or her own bedroom.
- Write a concluding paragraph in which you give miscellaneous details about what rooms in your home should have fire extinguishers, rope ladders, or other emergency equipment.
- Make a diagram of your house for each bedroom, and mark each bedroom's escape route on the diagram in a bright color so it can be easily seen.

When you finish the rough draft of your paper, ask a student who sits near you to read it. After reading your rough draft, he/she should tell you what he/she liked best about your work, which parts were difficult to understand, and ways in which your work could be improved. Reread your paper considering your critic's comments, and make the corrections you think are necessary.

PROOFREADING

Do a final proofreading of your paper, double-checking your grammar, spelling, organization, and the clarity of your ideas. Make a final, good copy to submit for grading.

NOTES
Fahrenheit 451

WRITING ASSIGNMENT 2
Fahrenheit 451
The Future World

PROMPT

Ray Bradbury wrote Fahrenheit back in 1951, yet his work is still very relevant today. It is amazing that he was able to foresee the progression of so many things so accurately. When he wrote this book, television had just been invented. There were no such things as "ear buds" or "ear phones." The world of micro-technology and computers had not yet been discovered.

No one really knows how things will be in the future, but at one time or another, we all think about it. What is your vision of the future? What do you think our world will be like 50 years from now?

Your assignment is to describe our world as you believe it will be 50 years from now.

PREWRITING
- Choose five major topics for your composition--five areas of our lives you will describe. Some areas to consider are government, ecology, business, lifestyle, transportation, jobs/workplaces, family, economy, food, shelter, clothing, music, architecture, agriculture, and entertainment, but don't feel limited by these; you may consider other areas as well.
- Make five columns on a piece of paper and title each with one of the five topics you have chosen. Under each topic, in the appropriate columns, jot down notes about how you think each will be in 50 years.

DRAFTING
- Write a paragraph in which you introduce the idea that you believe life will be different in 50 years, especially in the areas you have chosen to write about (your five topics).
- In the body of your composition, write one paragraph for each of your topics. Use a topic sentence to state exactly how you believe that topic will be different in 50 years, and then fill in your paragraph with specific examples from your column of notes. Do this for each of your five topics, one paragraph for each topic.
- Write a paragraph in which you summarize your ideas and conclude your composition.

When you finish the rough draft of your paper, ask a student who sits near you to read it. After reading your rough draft, he/she should tell you what he/she liked best about your work, which parts were difficult to understand, and ways in which your work could be improved. Reread your paper considering your critic's comments, and make the corrections you think are necessary.

PROOFREADING

Do a final proofreading of your paper, double-checking your grammar, spelling, organization, and the clarity of your ideas. Make a final, good copy to submit for grading.

NOTES
Fahrenheit 451

PERSUASIVE WRITING ASSIGNMENT
Fahrenheit 451
Which Is Better Now Or The Future?

PROMPT

Well, we know what it is like living in our world today. And now we have some ideas about how our future might be. Which one is better?

Your assignment is to convince me that either our world today is better than the future will be or that the future will be better than our world is today.

PREWRITING
- Decide for yourself which you think will be better: the present world or the world of the future.
- Write down three of the most important things that convinced you to make your decision.
- On a piece of paper, make two columns. Title one "Now" and title the other one "Future."
- Down the left-hand margin of your paper, leaving plenty of space in between, write down the three most important things that convinced you to make your decision in the paragraph above.
- Now fill in the little chart you have made. Consider the first thing. Write down how it is today in your "Now" column. Write down how it will be in the "Future" column.
- Do the same thing with each of the items in your far-left column.

DRAFTING
- Write a paragraph in which you introduce the idea that either today is better than the future or that the future is better than the present.
- In the body of your composition, write one paragraph for each of your main points. Take your first "most important thing that convinced you" and write a paragraph about that. Make a topic sentence in which you tell your reason why the "Now" or "Future" world will be better. Fill out your paragraph by comparing our world today with the future world on this point. (Use your chart.) Write one paragraph in this way for each of your three reasons.
- Write a concluding paragraph in which you summarize your ideas and conclude your composition.

When you finish the rough draft of your paper, ask a student who sits near you to read it. After reading your rough draft, he/she should tell you what he/she liked best about your work, which parts were difficult to understand, and ways in which your work could be improved. Reread your paper considering your critic's comments, and make the corrections you think are necessary.

PROOFREADING

Do a final proofreading of your paper double-checking your grammar, spelling, organization, and the clarity of your ideas. Revise to a final draft as necessary.

NOTES
Fahrenheit 451

WHOLE BOOK STUDY
Fahrenheit 451

ASSIGNMENTS AND ACTIVITIES
TO STUDY DIFFERENT ASPECTS
OF THE WHOLE BOOK

NOTES
Fahrenheit 451

HISTORICAL CONTEXT
Fahrenheit 451

In 1951 Ray Bradbury wrote a short story ("The Fireman") on which Fahrenheit 451 (published in 1953) was based. What was going on in Bradbury's world and in his mind to prompt him to create Montag's world? Take a few minutes to jot down some things that were going on between 1941-1953. Then, see which of these things you can make correlations to in Fahrenheit 451.

World Events:

_____
_____
_____
_____
_____
_____
_____

Entertainment:

_____
_____
_____
_____
_____
_____
_____

Science & Technology:

_____
_____
_____
_____
_____
_____

Social:

_____
_____
_____
_____
_____

Other:

_____
_____

Historical Context: Fahrenheit 451 Page 2

EVENT	EFFECT IN FAHRENHEIT 451

POINT OF VIEW
Fahrenheit 451

Point Of View

Point of View is the lens through which the story is told.

There are several different kinds of Point of View:
- **First Person:** Told by a character in the story using "I"
- **Third Person Limited:** Told by a character in the story
- **Third Person Omniscient:** Told by the author through a character in the story; all-knowing

Based on these descriptions, which do you think fits Fahrenheit 451? Why?
_____
_____
_____
_____
_____

Why is it important that the story is told from Montag's point of view?
_____
_____
_____
_____
_____
_____

STORY MAP
Fahrenheit 451

Tell what happens at each part of the story.

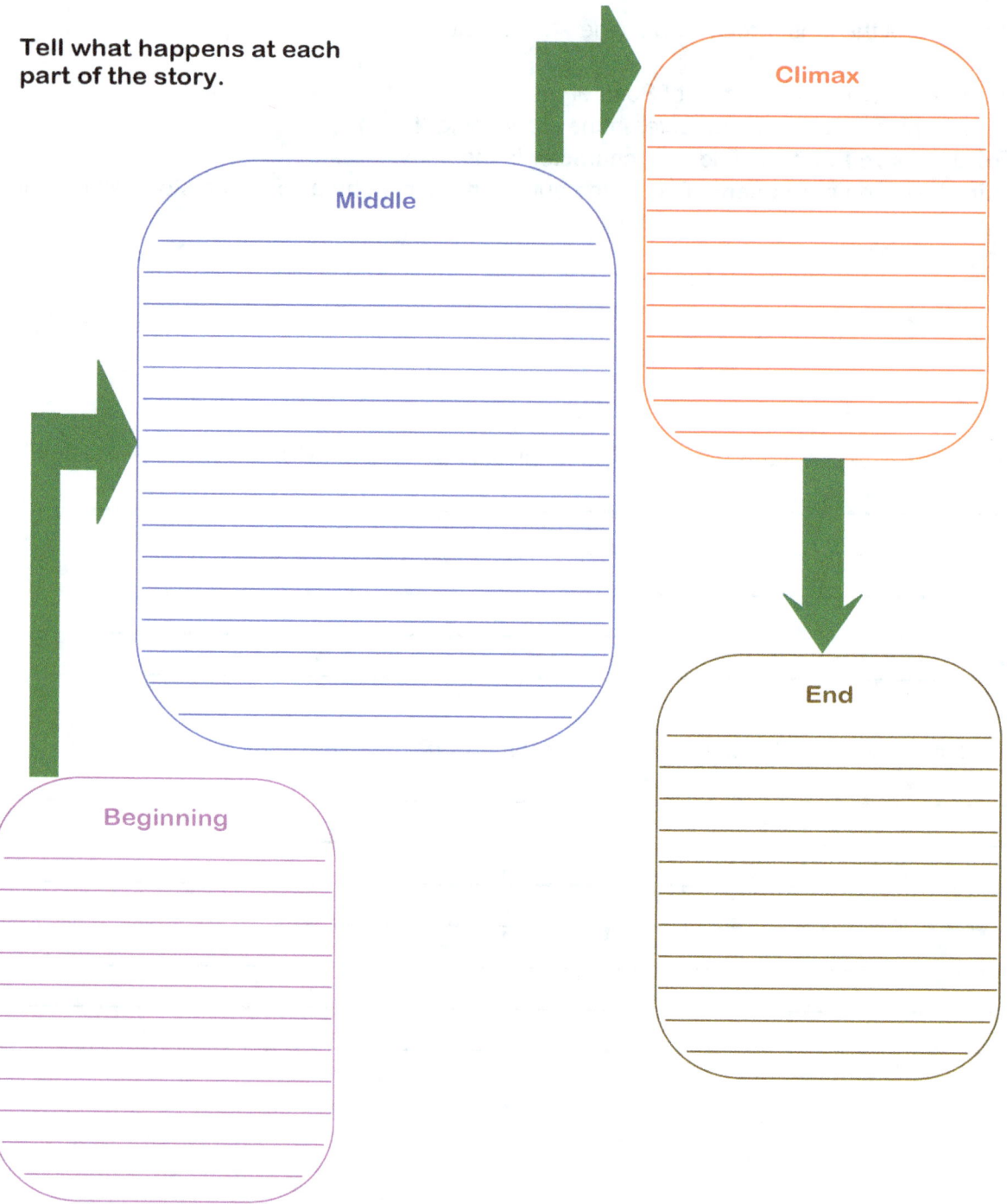

PLOT DIAGRAM
Fahrenheit 451

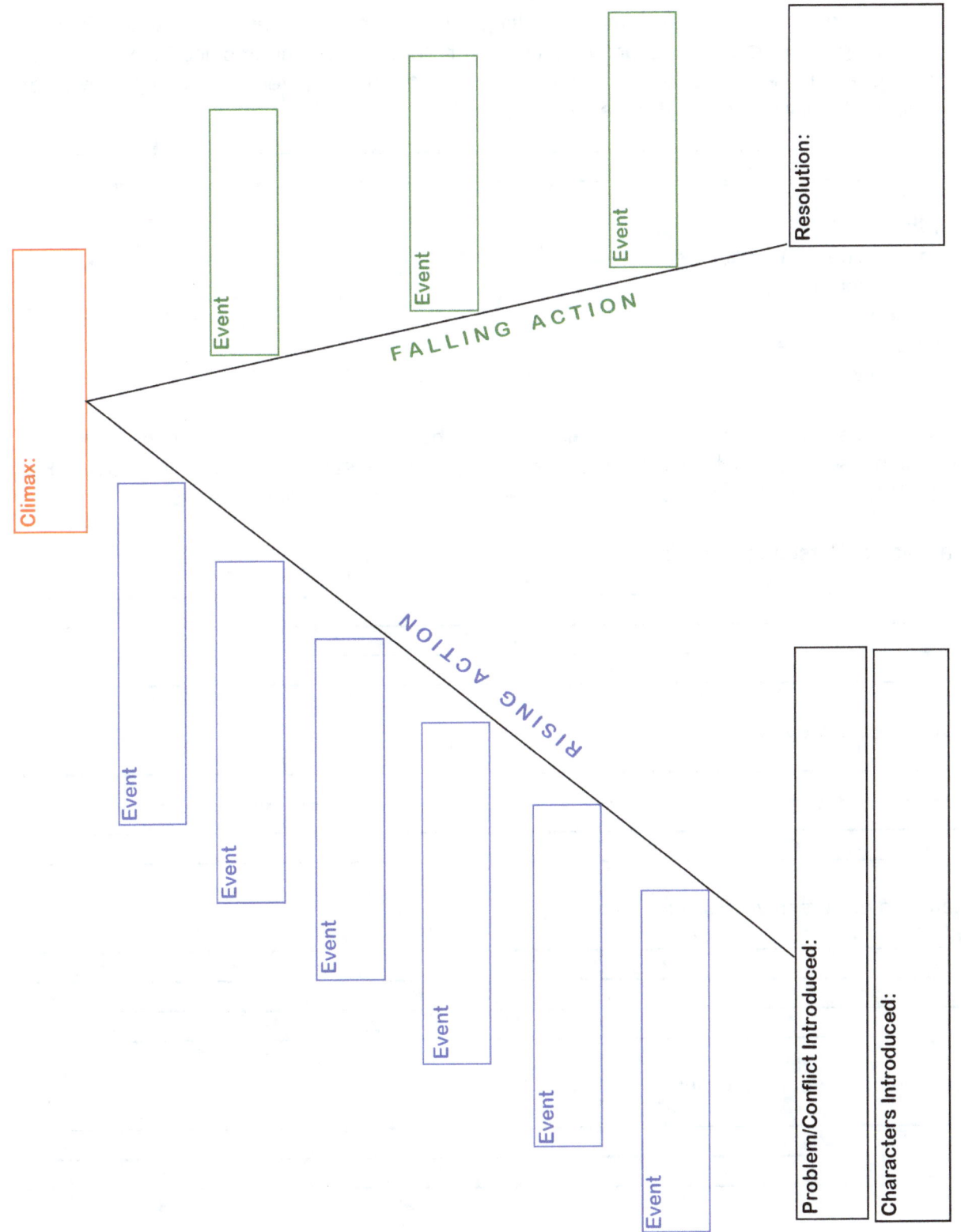

SETTING & CONFLICT
Fahrenheit 451

Setting
Though it is never stated, we assume the setting is in the United States, at some time in the future. Enough time has passed for two nuclear wars to have happened since the year 2022. Perhaps Bradbury set it 100 years into the future from 1950; it's never made completely clear, but it doesn't really matter what the exact year is. Why not?

_____
_____

Conflict
The basic types of conflict are:
- person vs. person
- person vs. self
- person vs. society
- person vs. nature

Main conflicts usually occur with the main character being the "person" against something. There can also be conflicts with other characters against the same elements. Think about Fahrenheit 451 and complete the exercise below with examples from Fahrenheit 451.

Examples of Person vs. Person

_____ vs _____
_____ vs _____
_____ vs _____
_____ vs _____

Examples of Person vs. Self

_____
_____
_____
_____

Examples of Person vs. Society

_____
_____
_____
_____

Examples of Person vs. Nature

_____
_____
_____

CHARACTER DEVELOPMENT
Fahrenheit 451

PART I: Character As An Element Of Fiction

1. Define "protagonist" _____

2. Define "antagonist" _____

3. The protagonist in Fahrenheit 451 is _____

4. The antagonist(s) in Fahrenheit 451 is/are _____

5. Define "dynamic character" _____

6. Define "static character" _____

7. What is a "stereotype"? _____

8. Which character in Fahrenheit 451 is dynamic? _____

9. Which characters in Fahrenheit 451 are static? _____
_____

10. Are any characters in Fahrenheit 451 stereotypes? If so, which ones?
_____

Below are the names of characters in Fahrenheit 451. On the blank to the left of each name, identify the person as having a major or minor role in the story. On the blank to the right of the name, identify the character

_____ Capt. Beatty _____

_____ Clarisse McClellan _____

_____ Granger _____

_____ Guy Montag _____

_____ Mildred _____

_____ Mrs. Black _____

_____ Elm St. Woman _____

_____ Mrs. Bowles _____

_____ Mrs. Phelps _____

_____ Professor Faber _____

_____ Stoneman and Black _____

CHARACTER DEVELOPMENT
Fahrenheit 451

PART 2: Character Studies - Beatty, Clarisse, Mildred, Faber, Mrs. Phelps

Beatty

1. List some of Beatty's physical characteristics.

   _____   _____   _____

2. What is one habit Beatty has that is symbolically important?

   _____

3. Find & list 5 events in Fahrenheit 451 in which what Beatty does or says is important.

   _____
   _____
   _____
   _____
   _____

4. Is Beatty *for* or *against* Montag? Support your answer with evidence from the book.

5. Montag thinks Beatty wanted to die. Do you agree or disagree with him? Use evidence from the book to support your answer.

CHARACTER DEVELOPMENT
Fahrenheit 451

PART 2: Character Studies - Beatty, Clarisse, Mildred, Faber, Mrs. Phelps

Clarisse

1. List some of Clarisse's physical characteristics.

_____   _____   _____

2. Give a few examples of the natural elements associated with Clarisse.

_____   _____   _____

3. What is the single most important question Clarisse asks Montag?

_____

    Why is that question important? What effect does it have on Montag?

_____
_____
_____
_____

4. What is the one thing about Clarisse that most attracts Montag to her? Tell *why* it attracts Montag to her.

_____
_____
_____

5. Explain why Clarisse's death is important in Fahrenheit 451.

_____
_____
_____
_____
_____
_____
_____

CHARACTER DEVELOPMENT
Fahrenheit 451

PART 2: Character Studies - Beatty, Clarisse, Mildred, Faber, Mrs. Phelps

Mildred

1. List some of Mildred's physical characteristics.

   _____   _____   _____

2. Choose one word or phrase you believe best sums-up Mildred's personality. Support your choice with examples from the text.

   _____
   _____
   _____
   _____
   _____
   _____
   _____

3. What are 3 things Mildred routinely does?

   _____
   _____
   _____

   What do these three things have in common, and what does that say about Millie?

   _____
   _____
   _____
   _____

4. Why does Mildred call in the alarm on her own house?

   _____
   _____
   _____
   _____
   _____

CHARACTER DEVELOPMENT
Fahrenheit 451

PART 2: Character Studies - Beatty, Clarisse, Mildred, Faber, Mrs. Phelps

Faber

1. List some of Faber's physical characteristics.

_____   _____   _____

2. Faber is a relatively minor character in Fahrenheit 451, but he is important. What function does Faber's character have in the story?

_____
_____
_____
_____
_____
_____

3. Give a verbal snapshot of Faber before Montag solicits his help and afterwards.

Before: _____
_____

After: _____
_____

4. Did Faber live at the end of the story? What evidence is in the text? Does it matter if Faber lives or dies at the end of the story?

_____
_____
_____
_____
_____
_____
_____

CHARACTER DEVELOPMENT
Fahrenheit 451

PART 2: Character Studies - Beatty, Clarisse, Mildred, Faber, Mrs. Phelps

Mrs. Phelps

1. List 5 of the most important things Mrs. Phelps says or does.

_____
_____
_____
_____
_____

2. Which of the 5 things you listed above gives us the most insight into Mrs. Phelps's character? Why?

_____
_____
_____
_____
_____

3. Compare and contrast Mrs. Phelps and Mildred.

Similarities: _____
_____
_____
_____

Differences: _____
_____
_____
_____

4. What is Mrs. Phelps's use as a character in the story?

_____
_____
_____

CHARACTER DEVELOPMENT
Fahrenheit 451

PART 3: Montag's Development Through The Book

1. Montag goes through a number of events that transform him from the obedient Fireman Montag into the Book Of Ecclesiastes. Give a brief explanation of how or why each listed event changed him.

EVENT	EFFECT OF THE EVENT ON MONTAG
Montag meets Clarisse	
Mildred's stomach is pumped	
Montag realizes he is not happy	
Mrs. Blake lights the fire	
Clarisse dies	
Montag realizes he does not love Millie	
Faber agrees to help	
Montag burns down his own house	
Beatty verbally assaults Montag and threatens to get Faber	
Montag meets Granger	

CHARACTER DEVELOPMENT
Fahrenheit 451

PART 3: Montag's Development Through The Book, page 2

2. In a work of fiction, the author can simply tell you about the character. That's called **Direct Characterization**.

In fiction, as in real life, we can also learn about the character
- through the character's physical appearance
- through the character's own words, thoughts, and actions
- through the comments of other characters

This is called **Indirect Characterization.**

Look through the text and find examples of each of these kinds of indirect characterization as they apply to Montag. Include the words from the text and, if not evident, what we learn about Montag from the example given.

Physical Appearance _____
_____
_____
_____

Character's Own Words _____
_____
_____
_____
_____

Character's Own Thoughts _____
_____
_____
_____
_____

Character's Own Actions _____
_____
_____
_____
_____

Comments Of Other Characters _____
_____
_____
_____
_____

CHARACTER DEVELOPMENT
Fahrenheit 451

PART 3: Montag's Development Through The Book, page 3

3. A character who changes has to be motivated by something. What is Montag's motivation to change? What does he want more than anything else, enough to lose his home, his wife, and his job? Support your answer with textual evidence.

_____

_____

_____

_____

_____

_____

_____

_____

4. Clarisse dies. Do you think Montag's development would have been different if Clarisse hadn't died? Explain.

_____

_____

_____

_____

_____

_____

5. Mildred is incapable of sharing Montag's journey. Do you think Montag's development would have been different if Millie had been able to share Montag's passion for finding a new life? Explain.

_____

_____

_____

_____

_____

_____

CHARACTER COMPARISON
Fahrenheit 451

Write Montag's traits on the top lines, Faber's on the bottom lines, and the traits the two characters have in common on the middle lines.

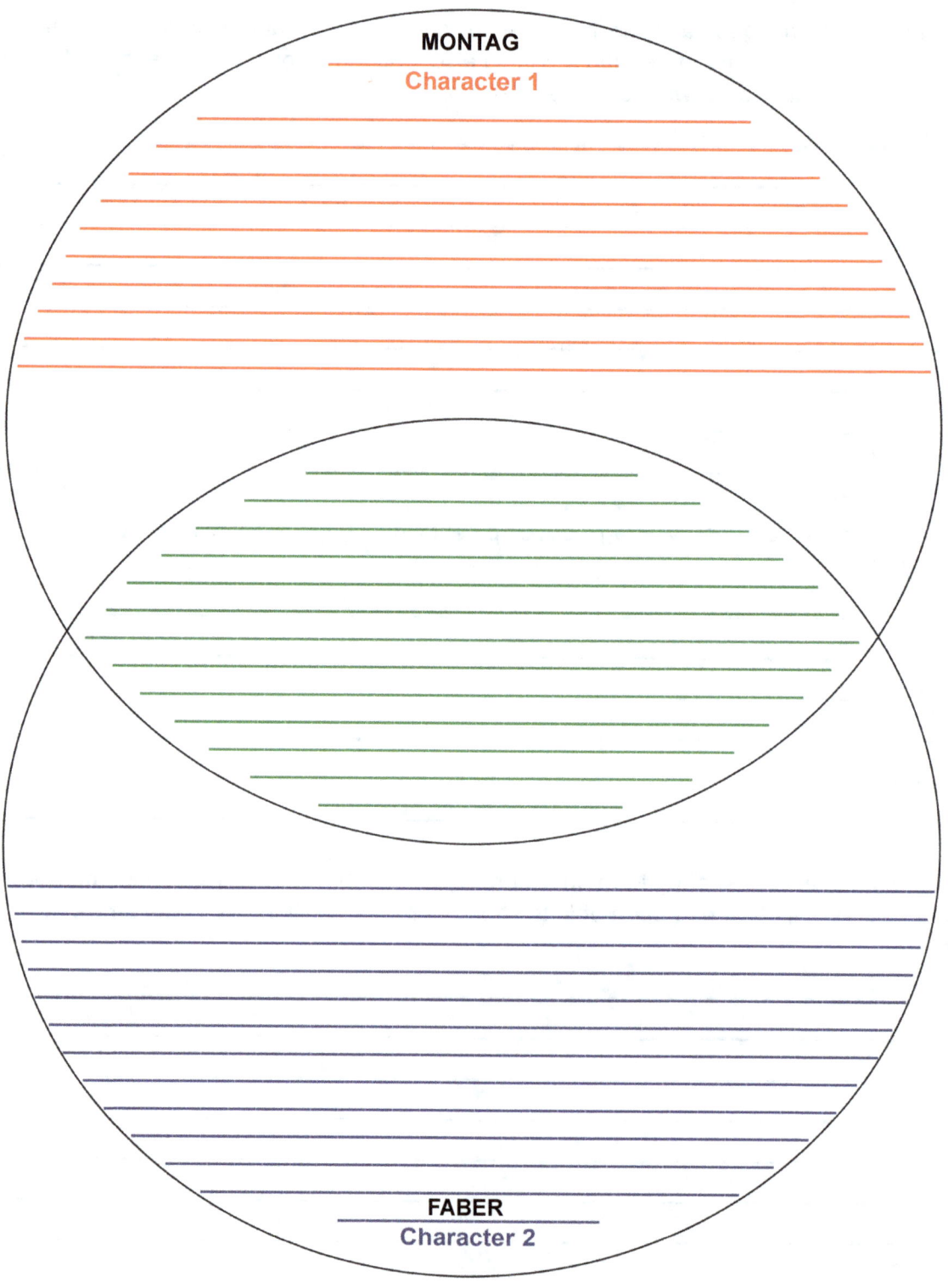

CHARACTER COMPARISON
Fahrenheit 451

Write Montag's traits on the top lines, Beatty's on the bottom lines, and the traits the two characters have in common on the middle lines.

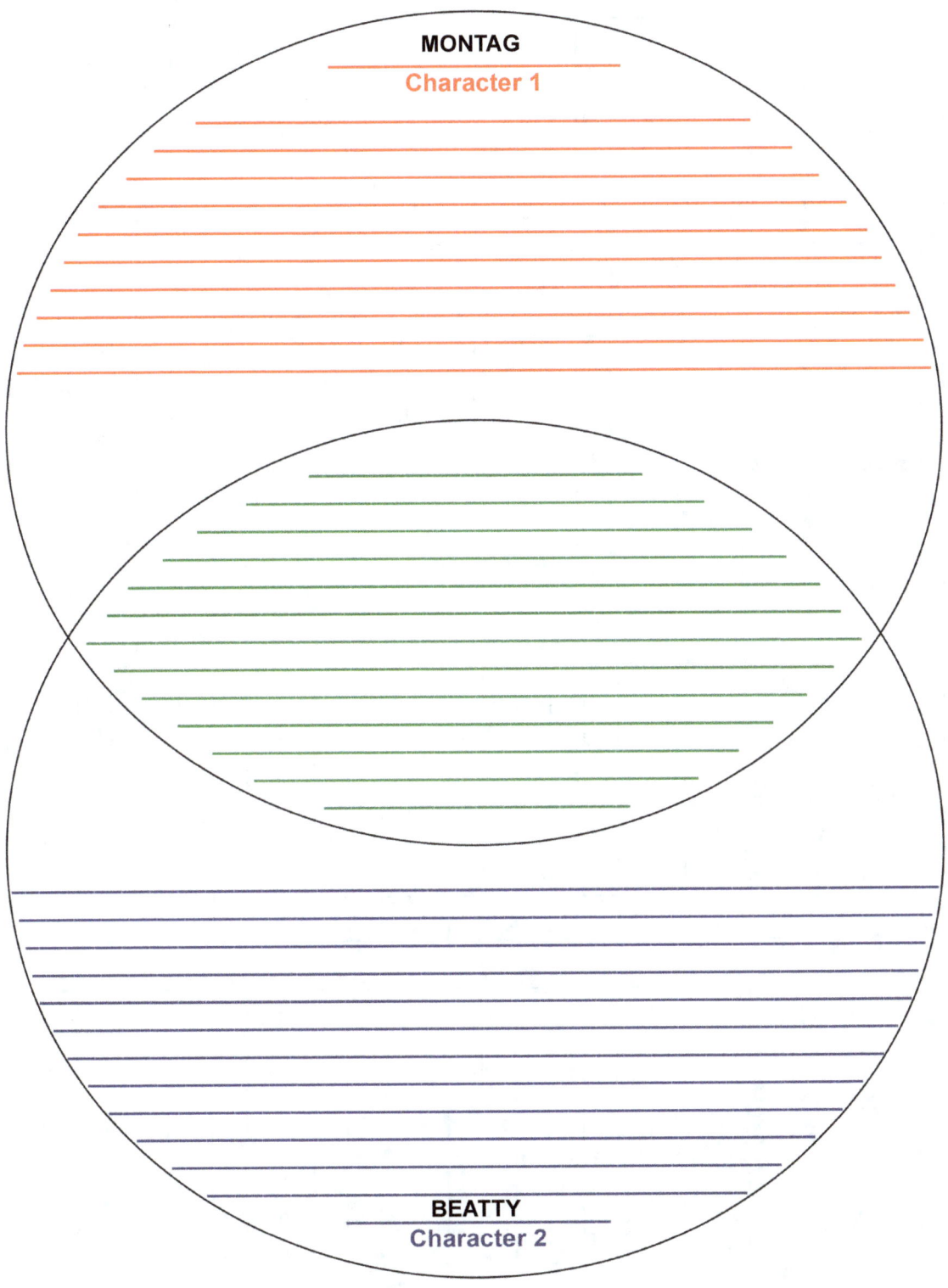

CHARACTER TRAITS: MONTAG
Fahrenheit 451

Choose 4 of Montag's character traits. Write one trait in each top box.
In the bottom boxes, note the evidence of that trait and the text page on which it is found.

CHARACTER TRAITS: MILDRED
Fahrenheit 451

Choose 3 of Mildred's character traits. Write one trait in each top box.
In the bottom boxes, note the evidence of that trait and the text page on which it is found.

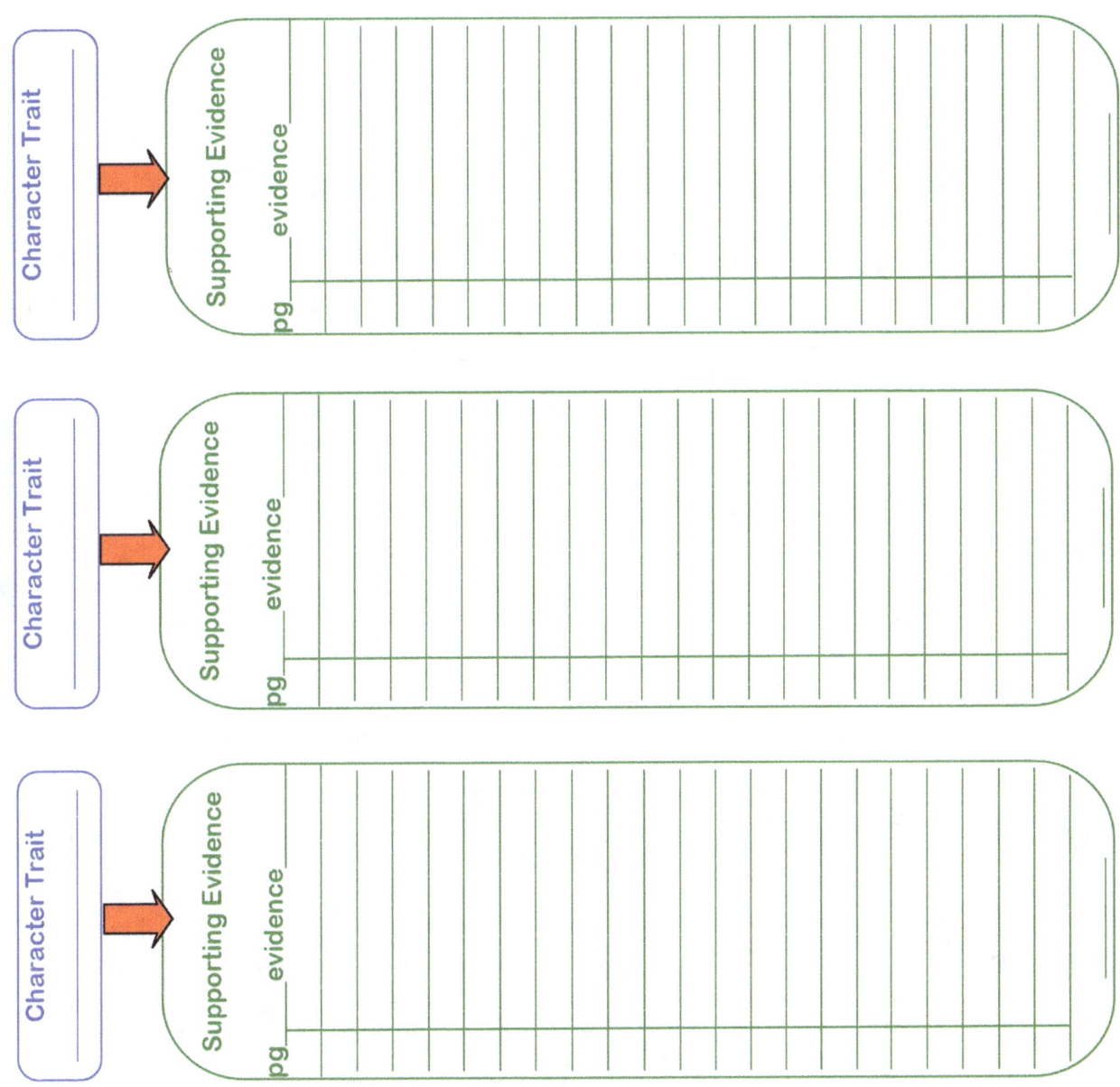

CHARACTER TRAITS: BEATTY
Fahrenheit 451

Choose 3 of Beatty's character traits. Write one trait in each top box.
In the bottom boxes, note the evidence of that trait and the text page on which it is found.

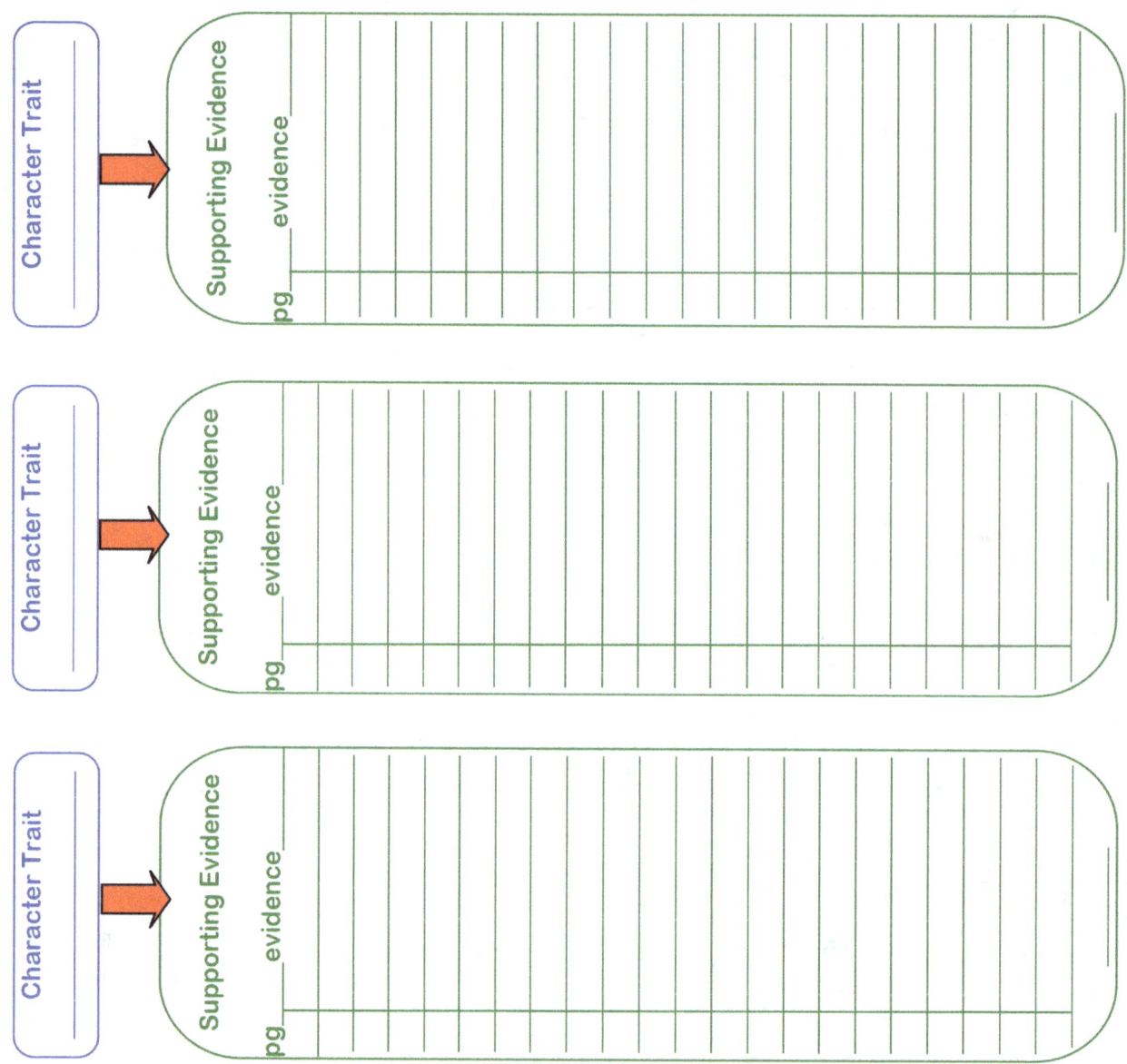

SYMBOLISM & IMAGERY
Fahrenheit 451

PART 1: The Chapter Titles
The passages below are about symbolism and the relevance of each chapter's title to the contents of the chapter and the book. Read these passages and answer the questions that follow.

The Hearth And The Salamander

A "hearth" is the brick or stone part of a fireplace that extends out into the room. Often the hearth is raised up from floor level, but it doesn't have to be. Sometimes "hearth" is used to refer to the fireplace as a whole.

In the days before other home heating methods and gas or electric stoves were available, big fireplaces with huge hearths were located in the kitchen or in the kitchen/living/dining room space. Family life centered around these hearths. Food would be cooked in kettles or pans that were heated by the fire. Dinner would be served at a table near the hearth, and after dinner family members would sit near the hearth to keep warm while reading, doing needlework, or conducting other activities. Because the hearth was so central to family life, it often is a symbol of "home."

Salamanders are amphibians. Like many frogs, they live in or near water or in other cool, damp places. In appearance, they resemble a lizard in form with skin more like a frog's in texture. Salamanders can be poisonous, so many are brightly colored to warn predators of their toxicity.

The important thing about salamanders, as far as their symbolic importance in Fahrenheit 451, is their association with fire. In ancient times, people thought salamanders were born from fire! Actually, they lived in rotten logs and when the logs were burned, the salamanders came out to escape the flames. For centuries people thought that salamander skin was fireproof and that salamanders could even put out fires.

In Fahrenheit 451 the fire trucks are called salamanders. Why? It's probably because of the ancient legends about salamanders coming from fire and being able to put out fires.

(continued on next page)

Symbols In Fahrenheit 451: Chapter Names, Page 2

But how do "hearth" and "salamander" go together to be an appropriate name for this chapter? Yes, the fire trucks are called salamanders but they carry firemen who start fires in homes; they don't put out fires. Consider that the salamander might represent something other than the firetrucks. To figure out what that might be, look at what the chapter is about.

Montag is the central character in this chapter, and he's a fireman. Therefore there's a good chance that he is somehow connected with this salamander symbolism. Salamanders were thought to be born from fire. Montag in his current occupation starts fires; fire is a big part of his life. Salamanders were thought to come out of the fire. Montag meets Clarisse and sees Mrs. Blake set fire to herself and her home--events which start to bring him away from (out of) his life of starting fires and into a state where he doesn't want to start fires anymore. In fact, he wants to stop the fires from being set. Hmmm. Salamanders were thought to put out fires. Are you seeing the connections? "Salamander" in the title refers to Montag. The new Montag comes from a life of fire and goes into a life of stopping fires, wanting the book and home burnings to stop.

So what does "hearth" have to do with any of this? Traditionally, as previously explained, "hearth" is a symbol of "home." Notice it isn't a symbol of "house." "Home" encompasses family, safety, warmth, and love; it is associated with tradition and roots, wholeness and togetherness.

In this chapter, Montag burns homes along with the books. Montag's own home is not "homey" at all; in fact, it is cold, almost sterile in nature. There's no warmth, no hearth, no good smells, no love, no togetherness, no sharing. Our salamander Montag sees the contrast between his own house and Clarisse's home, his own lifestyle and Clarisse's lifestyle--and realizes how empty his life is. He begins to want the emptiness of his life to be filled up.

So, The Hearth And The Salamander is a very appropriate name for this chapter. Montag, the salamander, is born from a life of fire. He is brought out of this life of fire through meeting Clarisse and realizing how empty his life is. He sees his own house is not a home and he begins looking for something that will satisfy his yearnings. He thinks books hold the answer. Burning books, burning homes, burning people becomes directly opposed to what Montag most wants; in fact, he wants the burning of books, homes, and people to stop. He becomes a catalyst, a force for the goal of stopping the fires.

(continued on next page)

The Sand And The Sieve

A sieve is a device, usually shaped like a shallow bowl or a tall cup, with holes punched in the bottom. The purpose of a sieve is to let smaller particles through the holes while retaining the larger parts, to separate the larger particles from the smaller ones.

The title of this chapter comes from Montag's remembering that as a child at the beach, a cousin offered him a dime if he would fill a sieve up with sand. The sand, of course, went right through the holes in the sieve. He tried and tried to fill it up, but he just couldn't do it. He sat there and cried.

What basically happens in chapter two? Montag remembers Faber, finds his address, and takes a book to him. While on the train, Montag realizes he'll have to give the book to Beatty very soon, so he tries to memorize it on the train ride to Faber's house. But he can't. The PA system on the bus is busy blaring an advertisement for Denham's Dentifrice, Denham's Dandy Dental Detergent. It's impossible to concentrate, to think, to remember with the ad blaring. He gets really frustrated and finally bursts out yelling for the thing to shut up. He tries to retain the words, but they slip through his mind like sand through a sieve.

That's one connection. But is it enough to name a whole chapter for it? What else goes on in the chapter? At this point in the novel, Montag has some knowledge: he knows he is unhappy; he has discovered some things that seem like a better way of life; he believes books hold the information he needs to find happiness and fulfillment. This is a great discovery, and he wants to share it with someone. He tries to share it with Millie and then with Millie and her friends, but they don't "get it." No matter how hard he tries to make them enlightened in the way he has become enlightened, they just don't "get it." He tries and tries to fill them up with these wonderful, new ideas but Millie and her friends are incapable of understanding or retaining the ideas he is trying to share with them, just like the sieve was incapable of holding the sand he tried to put in it.

Symbols In Fahrenheit 451: Chapter Names, Page 4

Burning Bright
The title of this chapter is a reference to a poem called "The Tyger" by William Blake:

> Tyger Tyger, burning bright,
> In the forests of the night;
> What immortal hand or eye,
> Could frame thy fearful symmetry?
>
> In what distant deeps or skies.
> Burnt the fire of thine eyes?
> On what wings dare he aspire?
> What the hand, dare seize the fire?
>
> And what shoulder, & what art,
> Could twist the sinews of thy heart?
> And when thy heart began to beat,
> What dread hand? & what dread feet?
>
> What the hammer? what the chain,
> In what furnace was thy brain?
> What the anvil? what dread grasp,
> Dare its deadly terrors clasp!
>
> When the stars threw down their spears
> And water'd heaven with their tears:
> Did he smile his work to see?
> Did he who made the Lamb make thee?
>
> Tyger Tyger burning bright,
> In the forests of the night:
> What immortal hand or eye,
> Dare frame thy fearful symmetry?

The idea is, "Who made the tiger, so beautiful on the outside, yet with such a fierce heart? And, was the maker pleased with his creation?" The connection to Fahrenheit 451 is "Who made mankind, so beautiful on the outside but so prone to all the things that lead to self destruction and war? And is the maker pleased with his creation?" Notice, too, that tigers' coats are orange and black and white--important colors in Fahrenheit 451: fire, evil, purity.

The chapter title is also appropriate literally: Montag's house is burned and Mildred leaves, freeing him from his past. Beatty and the Mechanical Hound are burned, in a sense freeing Montag from nagging and fear...and possibly foreshadowing the end of the society. The city burns in a bright flash of light, ending all mankind built into it and clearing the slate for a new beginning. As Beatty said, "Burn all, burn everything. Fire is bright and fire is clean."

SYMBOLISM & IMAGERY
Fahrenheit 451

PART 1: The Chapter Titles
Questions To Answer

1. The hearth is usually a symbol of _____.

2. People used to think that salamanders were born from _____ and were _____.

3. The title Burning Bright is a reference to _____.

4. Four things burn brightly in chapter three:
   _____
   _____
   _____
   _____

5. The _____ is a good symbol for Montag because _____

6. Mildred and her friends are like a _____ because they _____

7. While on the train, Montag yelled, "Shut up!" because _____

8. Montag's house is not a home because _____

ARTICLE EVALUATION
Fahrenheit 451

Reading & Evaluating Informational Texts

1. What is the purpose of the article? How well did it achieve this purpose?

_____
_____
_____
_____
_____

2. What is the central idea of the article?

_____
_____
_____

2. Are the points that are made logical; is the reasoning sound? Give an example or two.

_____
_____
_____
_____
_____

3. Are the points well developed? Explain why you think so or not.

_____
_____
_____
_____
_____

4. Do you think this article is well-done as-written, or do you think it should be revised to be better? What would make it better?

_____
_____
_____
_____
_____
_____
_____

SYMBOLISM & IMAGERY
Fahrenheit 451

PART 2: Symbols & Imagery Within The Text

There are many symbols within the text of Fahrenheit 451. Read about some of them below and then complete the exercise that follows.

Fahrenheit 451

Paper burns around 451 degrees Fahrenheit. This number isn't exact because the actual number depends on the chemical composition of the paper, moisture content, and so on. However, for the purposes of this novel, 451 is symbolic of the temperature at which book paper burns.

Snake Imagery

Here are some passages where the snake imagery is found:
- "One of them [the machines] slid down into your stomach like a black cobra down an echoing well...."
- "...a silly empty man near a silly empty woman, while the hungry snake made her still more empty."
- "There's a Phoenix car just drove up and a man in a black shirt with an orange snake stitched on his arm coming up the front walk."
- "I saw the damnedest snake in the world the other night. It was dead but it was alive. It could see but it couldn't see."
- "A voice drifted after him, 'Denham's Denham's Denham's,' the train hissed like a snake. The train vanished in its hole."

Traditionally, snakes are the bad guys--evil incarnate. This started with the story of Adam and Eve in the Garden of Eden in the Bible, when the Devil, disguised as a snake, tempted Eve to eat the forbidden fruit from the Tree of Knowledge.

In the passages above, the stomach-pumping machine is like a snake, Beatty has the symbol of a snake on his arm, and the train hisses like a snake. The need for stomach-pumping (and having it done in such a cold, uncaring manner like a janitorial mop-up), and the train's PA system's pounding noise and advertising at the occupants so they could think of nothing else are bad things in and for people, signs of an unhealthy society.

In the other three references noted, the snake represents whomever is creating the rules and pushing for this kind of lifestyle. Beatty is Captain of the firemen, definitely an enforcer of the rules. The hungry snake that "made her still more empty" is the society that has so emptied its citizens. And the snake that was dead but was alive--the stomach-pumping apparatus that looked inside Mildred to suck out all the junk--also could represent the seemingly intangible yet ever-present forces that created Montag's society. Rules and laws are not living things, yet they can suck the life out of the living by stripping people of the ability to think for themselves, by eroding freedom and choices, and by taking all the fun, creativity, and "meat" out of daily life.

Book Burning

Books are the traditional method of recording knowledge. Therefore, books represent knowledge and are the record of all the things people have thought, done, and imagined for all of recorded time. When there is no written record of something, it is easy to forget (as well as to modify) the facts. "Oh, that never *really* happened. Someone just made it up." "Firemen never put out fires; that's an old tale." In this sense, the burning of the books is symbolic of the new regime getting rid of the past so it can indoctrinate the people into believing what it wants them to believe.

Books hold ideas. Ideas spark imagination and creativity. They inspire people to think, to suppose, to wonder, and to want to find truth in life. If a regime wants to control people, to make people fall in line and do what they are told, books are the enemy and must be destroyed. Creativity, thinking, and questioning go against being controlled. Burning books can therefore also represent the destruction of creativity and thought as well as the emergence of the dominance of a regime attempting to control a population.

You might also note that in Fahrenheit 451, the firemen not only burn the books, they also burn the houses and relocate the residents to asylums or elsewhere. It isn't just about removing the books; it's about totally eliminating any opposition, anyone who might disagree or want things to be different.

Phoenix

Granger tells the story of the Phoenix, the bird that every few hundred years built a pyre and burned himself up and then rose again from the ashes to start anew. The image of the Phoenix is visible on Montag's chest when he meets Clarisse as well as on the Captain's hat and car. It is often a part of the symbology for firemen because of the Phoenix's destruction by fire.

When Granger tells about the Phoenix, he says it "must have been first cousin to Man....it looks like we're doing the same thing." This not only speaks to Mankind's past, it foreshadows the bombing of the city and the renewal that will occur afterwards.

Parlor Walls

In the past, homes often had rooms called parlors. These rooms were like a formal living room where family and guests would gather, often after dinner. Men would discuss politics, business, or other intellectual matters. A wife might do needlework or read; children were either not present or would sit and read or quietly play a game. At some point in the evening, a child or the wife might play the piano or provide some other kind of entertainment such as reciting, singing, or acting. Parlors were before television. If no guests were present, spouses might discuss family matters, neighborhood news, church or social club events, or the like.

In contrast, the Parlor Walls in Fahrenheit 451 are television on steroids; opposite in almost every way to the old-fashioned parlor. The walls are loud, colorful, and bright. Mildred is passive except for a few scripted lines she may have as "interaction." She takes in and is entertained by the sights and sounds on the big screens, but she never has to do or think anything. So it's ironic that Bradbury named them the "parlor" walls. One could make a case that Mildred meets her "family" and interacts with them in her Parlor Walls, but the "family" isn't real, and the shows don't have any substance.

This kind of mindless entertainment for hours on end is one part of the erosion of Mildred to emptiness. During the time of the Roman Empire, the politicians devised (and carried out) a plan to give the people cheap food and lots of entertainment so they would be happy and distracted from the political issues of the day, making their rise to power easier and practically uncontested. No one cared. "Give them bread and circuses" is the often-used phrase coined by Roman satirist and poet Juvenal. In the same way, Mildred and her friends don't really care about politics or much of anything except their shows. They don't even know or care why their country is at war.

The Parlor Walls, therefore, become symbolic of the ignorance and shallowness developed and encouraged by those in power to keep the masses of people happy and unconcerned with what the politicians are doing. It is also part of the metaphoric "hungry snake" that "made her [Mildred] still more empty."

Finally, Parlor Walls are also a means of escape for Mildred and her friends. Being entertained with happy and shallow programming, they can avoid facing the reality of their lives.

Seashells

Think of the "Seashells" as modern day ear buds. When Mildred isn't absorbed by the Parlor Walls, she is plugged in to her Seashells, being entertained by music or the radio. Before going to bed, she takes sleeping pills and plugs in her Seashells to drown out any thoughts of the day that will keep her awake. Like the Parlor Walls, they are a means of escape that promote lack of thought, and they are symbolic of the ignorance and shallowness encouraged by those in power.

The Green Bullet

So what about the Green Bullet, then? It's like a Seashell, isn't it? In form, yes, it is. It is a small, green, and bullet-shaped radio that fits into Montag's ear, as a Seashell would. But in substance it is quite different. Let's look at the name. What is green? Natural, living things like plants are green. But then there's that word "bullet," which usually is associated with killing, bringing death. What does the Green Bullet do? It provides a communications link between Faber and Montag, so Montag can have some help in responding to Beatty and others. Faber is a part of those with a green, "living" lifestyle--full of life, full of thoughts, real emotions, ideas, and creativity. Faber and Montag want to deliver a verbal bullet, a response that stops Beatty. In a larger sense, the Green Bullet becomes symbolic of finding a way to stop the erosion of humanity.

Fahrenheit 451 Symbols & Imagery Within The Text, Page 4

Mirrors

Look for a minute at the places where mirrors are used in the text:

- "He [Montag] knew that when he returned to the firehouse, he might wink at himself, a minstrel man, burnt-corked, in the mirror."
- "How like a mirror, too, her [Clarisse's] face. Impossible; for how many people did you know that refracted your own light back to you?"
- "These men [the firemen] were all mirror images of himself!"
- "There was a crash like the falling parts of a dream fashioned out of warped glass, mirrors, and crystal prisms." (as Mildred left the house in the beetle)
- "The look of you is enough. You haven't seen yourself in a mirror lately." (Granger to Montag)
- "...because in the millionth part of time left, she [Millie] saw her own face reflected there, in a mirror instead of a crystal ball, and it was such a wildly empty face, all by itself in the room, touching nothing, starved and eating of itself...."
- "Come on now, we're going to go build a mirror factory first and put out nothing but mirrors for the next year and take a long look in them."

That which is seen in a mirror is not real; it is a reflection of that which is real. Also, we cannot see ourselves without a mirror. We cannot see what we really look like without examining our own reflections. Go back and re-read the quotes above considering these ideas.

This whole book is filled with things that are real but not real, living but not living, seeming to be real but...not. The Mechanical Hound is mechanical, but it seems alive to Montag. The door-voice is not real, but it is personified. The "family" is not real, but Mildred treats them as if they are. The war is very real, but seems like it is not (until it's too late). History is real but is made into a fairy tale, a made-up story. These are just a few examples. Mirrors, reflections, distortions, and ironies abound in a close reading of Fahrenheit 451.

Think about this again: We cannot see what we really look like without examining our own reflections. This is physically true, but it also applies to our character. Without looking at our own actions, reflecting on the things we do, thinking about the effects of what we do and the meaning of what we do, we cannot know ourselves as individuals or as a society.

The Mechanical Hound

The Hound, like Beatty is a symbol of the establishment. In addition, the Hound represents the blurring of the non-living and living in Montag's world.

SYMBOLISM & IMAGERY
Fahrenheit 451

Part 2 Symbols & Images In The Text
Questions For Review

1. List 9 things that are important images or symbols in Fahrenheit 451:

   _____   _____   _____

   _____   _____   _____

   _____   _____   _____

2. Name three things or people that represent the establishment, those in control:

   _____   _____   _____

3. Name three things that are a means of "escape" for Mildred:

   _____   _____   _____

4. Years after people read Fahrenheit 451, the thing they remember is that it is about book burning. What does the book burning actually symbolize?

   _____
   _____
   _____
   _____
   _____

5. Why are the Parlor Walls important in Fahrenheit 451?

   _____
   _____
   _____

6. Explain how the story of the Phoenix relates to the city.

   _____
   _____
   _____
   _____

SYMBOLISM & IMAGERY
Fahrenheit 451

PART 3: Analyzing And Evaluating The Symbolic Use Of Rain: Assignment

Your assignment is to analyze and evaluate the symbolic use of rain in Fahrenheit 451.

- Find the passages where rain is mentioned and write them down (with page numbers). (Hint: If you have access to a digital form of the book, you can search "rain" to find passages then look them up in your book.)
- Skim before and after the passages to see what is happening in that part of the story.
- Look at the possible symbolic meaning rain might have in each passage & make notes about it.
- Review your notes about each passage and see what is in common.
- Draw conclusions based on your passage analysis.
- Write an analysis of the symbolic use of rain in Fahrenheit 451

A few observations about rain:
    Rain can be cleansing or renewing.
    Rainy/stormy weather can foreshadow bad things happening.
    Rain helps things grow.
    Rain is water, which is life-giving.

SYMBOLISM & IMAGERY
Fahrenheit 451

PART 3: Analyzing And Evaluating The Symbolic Use Of Rain: Notes

Page	Passage	Notes

SYMBOLISM & IMAGERY
Fahrenheit 451

PART 3: Analyzing And Evaluating The Symbolic Use Of Rain: Written Analysis

THEMES
Fahrenheit 451

There are many ways to approach studying the themes of Fahrenheit 451, but any approach has to start with the text, for it is through the text that the themes are developed.

You have already read the text from beginning to end. You may have looked at specific passages to consider the symbols within the story or to study character development. Let's pull out some things now that will help us understand the larger themes of the work.

Our study will be based on:
- Montag's Realizations
- Words & Actions Of Mildred And Her Friends
- Beatty's Commentaries
- Clarisse, Faber, & Granger's Contributions
- The Ending

Montag's Realizations

We all get pretty used to our own daily routines and our own way of life. We accept that what we do is how life *is*. That's how Montag is...until Clarisse slips into his world that evening on his way home from work. Her world is very different from his. It seems interesting to him. And she asks a simple question--almost as an afterthought before parting: "Are you happy?".

Montag goes home to find his wife in bed with her Seashells plugged into her ears. Motionless. Pale. Dull. None of which is unusual. In fact, he doesn't realize she has overdosed on sleeping pills until he kicks the empty bottle. The men come to pump out her stomach and fix her up, but their casual attitude toward this "clean up job" is annoying and upsetting to Montag. It doesn't take Montag long in the beginning of the novel to realize that he is *not* happy.

Then there's Clarisse. What is it about her that intrigues him? He likes talking with her. Unlike his wife, she is responsive and thoughtful, a breath of fresh air in his stale life. Again, it doesn't take Montag long to realize that he wants *that* kind of a life...one of conversation and thought and genuine interaction rather than thoughtless, automatic responses.

On top of all that, Montag witnesses a woman who is willing to die rather than live her life without her books. That's pretty powerful. Even more powerful is Montag's witnessing her light the match that starts the fire--and realizing that what he does for a living has real consequences for real people.

Montag realizes he is unhappy, realizes what kind of a lifestyle he wants, realizes that books have something that is important enough to die for, and realizes what he has been doing as a fireman is not such a great thing.

There's one more important realization. He can't share his new life quest with Millie. She's just not capable of understanding what he has discovered.

Fahrenheit 451: Themes, page 2

Words And Actions Of Millie And Her Friends

"Why?" we must ask, "Why is Mildred incapable of understanding and sharing Montag's quest for a new life?" The answer is pretty simple, really: she's just too shallow of a person. Montag reads to her, but the words have no meaning, they're just words. "It doesn't mean anything! The Captain was right!" she says. Then she is relieved to pick up the ringing telephone, to talk with her friend about the White Clown show.

Millie spends all of her time watching mindless shows on the Parlor Walls, listening to the radio through her Seashells, and talking with her friends about nothing in particular, the way her Parlor Wall "family" talks but says nothing of substance.

Children are a bother. No one in their right mind would want them. So ship them off to school to be taken care of by others. When they're home, plunk them in front of the Parlor Walls. There's a war, but no one knows why; it doesn't really matter. It happens somewhere else. Husbands go off to war and are expected back with no consequences. Elections are won on looks alone. Nothing that is troublesome or unpleasant is allowed in. Millie and her friends haven't a care in the world. In fact, Mildred says, "I am happy...and proud of it!"

How do Millie and her friends cope when things come into life that aren't so pleasant? They run away; escape to the Parlor Walls, the Seashells, the pills. They have no coping skills whatsoever. They are totally unprepared to meet real life. It overwhelms them. After the firetruck arrives at Montag's house, Mildred comes out...ignores Montag, like he is a stranger...talks to herself about the house as if it is someone else's...gets into the beetle and rides away.

Beatty's Commentaries

How did people become like Mildred...incapable of coping with reality? Ah, let's look back at Captain Beatty's commentaries and consider his words. Ironically, here is a condensed version of what Beatty says, with a whole bunch of stuff left out:

> "Whirl man's mind around about so fast under the pumping hands of publishers, exploiters, broadcasters that the centrifuge flings off all unnecessary, time-wasting thought! ... School is shortened, discipline relaxed, philosophies, histories, languages dropped....Life is immediate, the job counts, pleasure lies all about after work. ... Empty the theaters save for clowns and furnish the rooms with glass walls and pretty colors running up and down the walls.... More sports for everyone, group spirit, fun, and you don't have to think, eh? ... More pictures. The mind drinks less and less. Impatience. Highways full of crowds going somewhere, somewhere, somewhere, nowhere. ... Don't step on the toes of the dog-lovers, the cat-lovers, doctors, lawyers, merchants, ... There was no dictum, no declaration, no censorship, to start with, no! Technology, mass exploitation, and minority pressure carried the trick.... Today, thanks to them, you can stay happy all the time...."

> "We must all be alike. Not everyone born free and equal, as the Constitution says, but everyone made equal. Each man the image of every other; then all are happy, for there are no mountains to make them cower, to judge themselves against. ... A book is a loaded gun in the house next door. ... Who knows who might be the target of the well-read man?"

Fahrenheit 451: Themes, page 3

> "... Ask yourself, What do we want in this country, above all? People want to be happy....Well, aren't they? Don't we keep them moving, don't we give them fun? That's all we live for, isn't it? For pleasure, for titillation? ..."

> "Colored people don't like *Little Black Sambo*. Burn it. White people don't feel good about *Uncle Tom's Cabin*. Burn it. Someone's written a book on tobacco and cancer of the lungs? The cigarette people are weeping? Burn the book. ... Funerals are unhappy and pagan? Eliminate them, too. ... Burn all, burn everything. Fire is bright and fire is clean."

> "...So bring on your clubs and parties, your acrobats and magicians, your daredevils, jet cars, motorcycle helicopters, your sex and heroin, more of everything to do with automatic reflex."

And there you have it. That's basically how Beatty says the Mildreds and their friends came to be.

Clarisse, Faber, & Granger's Contributions
But the figurative door is left open, you see, because of Clarisse, Faber, Granger, and folks like them. Not *everyone* fell into the automatic reflex, always-happy trap. There are still people who like to have conversations and stand around, kicking leaves and thinking (Clarisse). There are still people who know that what has happened isn't a good thing, though they don't have the courage or the wherewithal to take action to change things on their own (Faber). There are still people who know, appreciate, and try to save that which has been burned, that which has been lost (Granger). And there are still people like Montag who say, "Hey! I want something more than this shallow, pretend-happy life."

The End
And in the end of the book, what happens? The shallow life Mankind acquiesced to over time brought itself down--and the outcasts, the thinkers, the do-ers, the people who could cope with reality, stepped in to start civilization anew.

Fahrenheit 451: Themes, page 4

Theme Notes

Use this page to jot down notes about theme in Fahrenheit 451.

1. Montag makes these important realizations:

- _____
- _____
- _____
- _____
- _____

2. Mildred is incapable of being a part of Montag's quest for a new lifestyle because

_____

3. Mildred and her friends can't cope with unpleasant realities. When they are faced with such things, their response is to _____ by turning to _____, _____, or _____.

4. Beatty gives a long speech stating how he thinks their society came to be as it is. Towards the end he says: "...So bring on your clubs and parties, your acrobats and magicians, your daredevils, jet cars, motorcycle helicopters, your sex and heroin, more of everything to do with _____ _____."

5. Not *everyone* fell into the automatic reflex, always-happy trap. There are still people who like to have conversations and stand around, kicking leaves and thinking (_____).

There are still people who know that what has happened isn't a good thing, though they don't have the courage or the wherewithal to take action to change things on their own (_____).

There are still people who know, appreciate, and try to save that which has been burned, that which has been lost (_____).

And there are still people like _____ who say, "Hey! I want something more than this shallow, pretend-happy life."

6. At the end of the book, the shallow life Mankind acquiesced to over time _____--and the outcasts, the thinkers, the do-ers, the people who could cope with reality, stepped in to _____.

Fahrenheit 451: Themes, page 5

From Text To Theme
We have looked at the text in a "big picture" way. Now, how do we get from this to that elusive thing called "theme"?

First we need to know what "theme" is.
Theme is the central idea of the book. It is the comment the book makes about life.
- Theme addresses the nature of humanity
- Theme addresses the nature of society
- Theme addresses the nature of humankind's relationship to the world and/or
- Theme addresses the nature of our ethical responsibilities

What is the nature of humanity as set forth in Fahrenheit 451?

_____

What is the nature of society as set forth in Fahrenheit 451?

_____

What is the nature of humankind's relationship to the world in Fahrenheit 451?

_____

What is the nature of our ethical responsibilities as set forth in Fahrenheit 451?

_____

All of that being said, and considering the "big picture" of the text that we have just examined, write one phrase or sentence that best states the main theme of Fahrenheit 451.

_____

_____

Are there other themes that are not the main theme? Did you have to choose among several things to determine the main theme? What other themes are in Fahrenheit 451?

_____

_____

_____

_____

Fahrenheit 451: Themes, page 6

Theme In Context

You've read the book and by studying it and getting to the theme, you know what it is really about, not just the story line. The next question to ask is, "Why?". Why would Ray Bradbury back in 1950 put pen to paper to write this book? And what did he intend for his readers to get from it? In a sense, the "theme" is what we get from the book, but until we turn that into his advice for us, his efforts are in vain, worthless.

<u>Why Did He Write It?</u>
Think about Ray Bradbury's lifetime. (He was born in 1920 and died in 2012.) His childhood took place in the Roaring Twenties, followed by the Great Depression, WWII, the rise of Communism, and the Korean War. In his lifetime, technological advances were astounding. Any thoughtful person would look at the world and wonder where all this would lead, as did Ray Bradbury.

Bradbury's book is a cautionary story, warning people of the possible consequences of the direction he saw the country going.

<u>What Would Ray Bradbury's Advice Be To Us, His Readers?</u>
Think about Fahrenheit 451 and all that is in it. Think about the characters, the themes, the ideas presented and discussed. Make a list of items of advice Ray Bradbury would give to you.

Do These Things:

_____
_____
_____
_____
_____
_____
_____
_____

Don't Do These Things:

_____
_____
_____
_____
_____
_____
_____
_____

Fahrenheit 451: Themes, page 7

Now you have a decision to make: you need to decide if this is good advice or not. It might all be good advice, some might be good and some not so good, or it all could be bad advice. What do you think? Is Bradbury's advice good or not? Answer completely below, explaining your answer fully.

_____
_____
_____
_____
_____
_____
_____
_____
_____
_____
_____
_____
_____
_____

It is wise to take good advice, and we usually benefit from that in the long run. If you believe any of Mr. Bradbury's advice is good, think for a few minutes how that might apply to you. Make a list of things you should probably stop doing and things you should probably start doing to act upon the advice given.

Start Doing These Things:

_____

_____

_____

_____

_____

Stop Doing/Do Less Of These Things:

_____

_____

_____

_____

_____

Anytime someone gives you advice, you have to evaluate it. Decide if it is good advice or not, and then act accordingly. Consider the source, think about the consequences of following the advice, and evaluate what that might mean for you.

ACTIVITY: EXPLORATION OF ADDITIONAL THEMES
Fahrenheit 451

The idea of total governmental control over an apathetic people and the censorship that goes along with that are not the only two themes in Fahrenheit 451. Some of the others include:

- knowledge versus ignorance
- the natural order & elements of the world versus a man-made world
- the blurring of the lines between animate and inanimate objects
- religion, religious imagery, and scriptural references
- conscious versus subconscious, often shown by hands acting on their own

This is not an exhaustive list, but it does hit many of the highlights of themes and motifs in the novel.

Your assignment is to fully explore one of these themes in Fahrenheit 451.

Here's to go about doing this assignment:
You will scan the text for references to this theme and note the references on the chart on the following page. Your group should assign each person in the group one of the reading assignment sections to scan for references to your theme.

When you finish noting references, you should come back together as a group to discuss each of the references you have found and try to draw some conclusions about the cumulative meaning of the references. Write these down in a few sentences at the bottom of the Notes page.

When all groups have completed these tasks, the class will come back together as a whole to share information and discuss each theme/motif that has been explored. Be prepared to share your information with the whole class.

After your textual research is over, you should find and read at least two articles written by others about your assigned theme or motif in the novel.

Finally, each group member should write a summary about your theme or motif, clearly stating what your theme or motif is and explaining its use in the novel, using specific examples from the text to support your statements and including (and citing) any appropriate information from the additional articles you read.

THEME/MOTIF NOTES
Fahrenheit 451

Theme/Motif _____

PAGE	REFERENCE

Use an additional sheet of notebook paper if needed for more references.

Notes About Cumulative Meaning Of The References:

_____
_____
_____
_____
_____
_____
_____

USE OF LANGUAGE
Fahrenheit 451

Writing is often referred to as a "craft." You may hear authors say they've spent years working on their craft. Well, a "craft" is an occupation that requires special skills or particular attention to details. A woodworker, for example, may craft a fine piece of furniture, taking great time and effort to make every joint, every angle, every carved detail perfect. The same is true with writing: authors take a great deal of time and effort to make every word, every sentence, every chapter fit the purposes of their book perfectly. Ray Bradbury was a master at this.

We can't look at every passage in the whole book; there just isn't enough time. But we can look at a few passages that show Mr. Bradbury's mastery very well, then you can go on to look at other passages on your own to truly appreciate his finely crafted work. At some point you should go back and reread the novel from start to end after completing this study. You will see so many things you missed the first time around.

Let's take a look at the beginning of the book.

Passage	Commentary
It was a pleasure to burn.	What? A *pleasure* to burn? How odd! It grabs our attention, lets us know something unusual is going on, & lets us know this person *likes* burning things. It introduces a main element of the book: burning.
It was a special pleasure to see things eaten, to see things blackened and *changed*.	Why "eaten" instead of "burned"? "Eaten" is much more graphic; it personifies the fire, right away giving lifelike qualities to an inanimate thing, introducing the theme of "living but not living, inanimate but perceived as alive" paradox in the book. "Changed" is in italics; this whole book is about change of one kind or another.
With the brass nozzle in his fists, with this great python spitting its venomous kerosene upon the world, the blood pounded in his head, and his hands were the hands of some amazing conductor playing all the symphonies of blazing and burning to bring down the tatters and charcoal ruins of history.	Calling the hose a python brings it to life & begins the snake imagery often used in the book. "Blood pounding in his head" graphically tells us he's excited, working hard, energized. The element of "hands" often used throughout the book is introduced. Who would think to liken using a fire hose to conducting a symphony? What are tatters? They are torn pieces; bits of shredded clothing. What does "to bring down the tatters and charcoal ruins of history" mean? It brings a mental image of old charred buildings falling down but we know it's more than that. How do you "bring down" or destroy history?! Yet, that is also an important element in the book. Remember how Montag was told firemen never put out fires; that was just an old tale? That is shredding history, turning history into charcoal ruins. And here it is at the very start of the book!

Fahrenheit 451: Use Of Language, page 2

Passage	Commentary
With his symbolic helmet numbered 451 on his stolid head, and his eyes all orange flame with the thought of what came next, he flicked the igniter and the house jumped up in a gorging fire that burned the evening sky red and yellow and black.	Bradbury *tells* us 451 is symbolic; he leaves no doubt. Montag's head is "stolid": not easily stirred or moved mentally; unemotional. One word introduces the unemotional, lethargic, passive nature of people in this society. When you look at someone's eyes, you can tell a lot about them. Montag's are all orange flame. Orange is a bright color, a warning color, as in a yellow/orange light of a traffic light or "road work ahead" signs--fire. Danger. The house "jumped up." That's personification (giving inanimate objects human qualities). Again, very graphic. It's a "gorging" fire; "gorging," as in gorging on a meal--feasting; overeating (which brings back the eating image from the previous paragraph). The fire "burned the evening sky red and yellow and black"--the sky (nature) is being burned (destroyed), another subtheme in the book...humankind's unnatural existence in the city. Red and yellow and black--colors of danger and evil.
He strode in a swarm of fireflies. He wanted above all, like the old joke, to shove a marshmallow on a stick in the furnace, while the flapping pigeon-winged books died on the porch and lawn of the house. While the books went up in sparkling whirls and blew away on a wind turned dark with burning.	"Fireflies" gives a living quality to the bits of glowing embers in the air, which are not alive. The idea of shoving a marshmallow on a stick in the furnace refers to toasting a marshmallow on a stick over a fire, but the idea has degenerated through the years. People no longer have campfires, so they relate to doing it via the furnace, which is something they *do* have. And, it's an old joke now, not something that people really used to do. History has been changed, and it makes no sense, so it's a joke. Again, there's more personification with the flapping pigeon-winged books dying on the porch and lawn, as if they had life and they were being killed. Why pigeon-winged instead of some other bird? Carrier pigeons carry messages, as books do. The book sparks blow away on a "wind turned dark,"...wind (nature) turned dark (perverted) with burning.
Montag grinned the fierce grin of all men singed and driven back by flame.	Why does Montag "grin," and why is it a "fierce" grin? A "grin" is a broad smile, usually to show pleasure. "Fierce," in this case, is as in a *fierce* competition: furiously eager or intense. He's loving what he does and is right in there giving it his all. Notice, too, that he is the same as "all men singed..." and later in the book he realizes he looks like all the other firemen.

Fahrenheit 451: Use Of Language, page 3

Passage	Commentary
He knew that when he returned to the firehouse, he might wink at himself, a minstrel man, burnt-corked, in the mirror. Later, going to sleep, he would feel the fiery smile still gripped by his face muscles, in the dark. It never went away, that smile, it never ever went away, as long as he remembered.	Winking at oneself is usually an indication of happy self-congratulations. The minstrel-man image is one of being someone other than who you appear to be, doubly appropriate because minstrel-men often performed in "black face," with their white faces artificially blackened--and the firemen have sooty, blackened faces. The mirror introduces the idea of self-examination, mirrors, reflections, and crystals that appear throughout the book. His smile never went away. He, like others in his society, are perpetually happy, and he can't remember not having that smile. Remember, though, that he laughs when he doesn't know how to respond to Clarisse--and that is an auto-response laugh, not because she says anything funny. Perhaps this perpetual smile is an auto-response, too…just always there. And, finally, it says, "as long as he remembered," not "as long as he could remember." We usually say we've been doing something as long as we can remember. One reading of this last line could beg the question, "As long as he remembered *what*?".

And yet, when we read these passages for the first time, it just seems like a regular beginning of a story. Little do we suspect that Mr. Bradbury has given us such a thorough introduction to the book and has packed all of this symbolism and imagery into a few short paragraphs. *That* is use of language, professionally crafted.

Ray Bradbury doesn't just tell a story. He manipulates us, his readers, by careful use of language to tap into our emotions and to bring images to mind. This is what brings the story to life; we see things in our mind. We can *see* Montag holding a python hose and those poor little books flapping as they die on the porch.

Fahrenheit 451: Use Of Language, page 4

Now it's your turn. Read the passage in the left column then create a commentary about the use of language in the passage, as was done above.

Passage	Commentary
The autumn leaves blew over the moonlit pavement in such a way as to make the girl who was moving there seem fixed to a sliding walk, letting the motion of the wind and the leaves carry her forward. Her head was half-bent to watch her shoes stir the circling leaves. Her face was slender and milk-white, and in it was a kind of gentle hunger that touched over everything with tireless curiosity. It was a look, almost, of pale surprise; the dark eyes were so fixed to the world that no move escaped them. Her dress was white and it whispered. He almost thought he heard the motion of her hands as she walked, and the infinitely small sound now, the white stir of her face turning when she discovered she was a moment away from a man who stood in the middle of the pavement waiting.	

Fahrenheit 451: Use Of Language, page 5

Figurative Language

In the passages above, some inanimate objects were given qualities of living things--the python (hose) spitting its venomous kerosene upon the world, for example. This is an example of figurative language called *personification*. There are many kinds of figurative language an author can use to craft his work. Here are a few:

Personification: Giving inanimate objects qualities of living things

Hyperbole: Exaggerating or making an overstatement

Metaphor: Comparing two unlike things without using *as* or *like*

Simile: Comparing two unlike things using *as* or *like*

Understatement: Opposite of hyperbole; emphasizing something by significantly lessening its degree

Here are some examples from Fahrenheit 451:

Personification:
- ...the flapping pigeon-winged books died on the porch...
- A fountain of books sprang down upon Montag...

Hyperbole:
- He felt his chest chopped down and split apart.
- I don't know anything anymore...

Metaphor:
- ...her eyes were two miraculous bits of violet amber...
- People were more often...torches, blazing away until they whiffed out. (This is sort-of a trick one. In the book it says "he searched for a simile" but what he actually used was a metaphor. If he had said "People were more often...*like* torches..." it would have been a simile.)
- The woman on the bed was no more than a hard stratum of marble...

Simile:
- How like a mirror, too, her face.
- ...she was like the eager watcher of a marionette show...
- Her face was like a snow-covered island upon which rain might fall...
- [The Mechanical Hound] was like a great bee come home from some field where the honey is full of poison wildness...

Understatement:
- The breath coming out the nostrils was so faint it stirred only the furthest fringes of life, a small leaf, a black feather, a single fiber of hair.
- A fountain of books sprang down upon Montag as he climbed shuddering up the sheer stairwell. How inconvenient!

Fahrenheit 451: Use Of Language, page 6

Figurative Language Exercise

How many examples of figurative language can you find in Fahrenheit 451? Jot them down and identify the type of figurative language for each (as well as the page number in the text) in the chart below.

Type = personification, hyperbole, metaphor, simile, or understatement

Type	Page	Example

FIGURATIVE LANGUAGE
Fahrenheit 451

This page tells you about different kinds of figurative language and gives examples. On the second page, write in an example of each kind that you can find in the text of Fahrenheit 451.

Kinds Of Figurative Language

irony — Use of words to express something different from and often opposite to their literal meaning
Sitting in school on a lovely spring day is my favorite thing to do.

onomatopoeia — Use of words that imitate the sounds associated with the things they refer to
buzz, splash, pop

simile — A comparison using the words "like" or "as"
smart like a fox growing like a weed as pretty as a picture

hyperbole — Extreme exaggeration used to describe a person or thing
She had as many pairs of shoes as there are stars in the sky.

metonymy — One word or phrase is substituted for another with which it is closely associated
Using "the sword" to indicate military power

personification — Attributing human qualities to inanimate objects, animals, or ideas
The wind howled. The trees nodded in agreement.

cliché — An expression that has been used repeatedly and has lost its appeal
as white as snow eat like a bird

metaphor — A comparison without the words *like* or *as*
The cat is a bag of bones.

paradox — A seemingly self-contradictory statement that has some truth to it
Standing is more tiring than walking.

FIGURATIVE LANGUAGE
Fahrenheit 451

Write in an example of each kind of figurative language that you can find in the text of Fahrenheit 451.

UNIT CROSSWORD
Fahrenheit 451

UNIT CROSSWORD CLUES
Fahrenheit 451

ACROSS
1. Condensed version of a book
5. Remains after burning
7. Small communications device used by Montag & Faber
9. Clarisse was killed by one
10. It smelled like perfume to Montag
12. What we do with books
15. Flames
18. Where Montag went after fleeing Faber's house
19. She liked to think and talk
22. Rising from the ashes
24. Destroy with flames
25. He wanted a more meaningful lifestyle
26. Faber's destination: St. ____
27. Time when most fires were set
28. To get away

DOWN
1. Stop living
2. Place where radio transmitter was put for use
3. Place where Montag met Faber
4. Rain tasted like this beverage
6. Mechanical ____
8. He helped Montag
11. Montag's path to safety
13. Not bound
14. ____ Hound
16. Flame starter
17. Mildred took an overdose of sleeping ___
20. Montag took a book from the Elm woman's ___
21. Ear thimbles
23. They memorized literature
24. Captain of the firemen

VOCABULARY CROSSWORD
Fahrenheit 451

VOCABULARY CROSSWORD CLUES
Fahrenheit 451

ACROSS
1 With a rhythmic flow
6 A pile of combustible materials for burning a corpse
7 The study of the dynamics of projectiles
12 Arousing strong dislike or displeasure
14 Returning like for like, especially evil
17 Having many faces or sides
18 Those who flaunt their knowledge
19 Sadness; gloominess

DOWN
2 Fine; small in diameter
3 Authoritative pronouncement
4 Bizarre; distorted
5 Not readily noticed or seen; not commonly known
8 Described
9 Italian herb
10 Ignoble fear in the face of danger
11 Apparatus consisting of a compartment spun around a central axis
13 Having or revealing little emotion
15 Relating to the sense of touch
16 Set up; established

NOTES
Fahrenheit 451

www.ingramcontent.com/pod-product-compliance
Lightning Source LLC
Chambersburg PA
CBHW081452070526
44586CB00019B/2319